The Painted Cake

To P, A, and G

The Painted Cake

Natasha Collins

Skyhorse Publishing

Contents

Welcome to The Painted Cake

I think it was inevitable that I would end up painting on cakes for a living: I hail from a long line of both artists and bakers, and so perhaps it was only a matter of time before someone in my family had the flash of inspiration to combine the two. Both of my parents are working artists, and they always encouraged me to take up my own brush. I admit, I did flirt briefly with the idea of becoming a dentist, but by the time I was fifteen I realised it wasn't for me, and my mother's sigh of relief was poorly hidden. (I should add that she has nothing against dentists, but even back then she could see I was more suited to artistic pursuits.) Instead, I trained as an illustrator and then somehow fell into textile design, where I stayed for nearly ten years.

But baking remained in my blood. My paternal grandmother was a great Lancashire baker (I still remember the taste of her fabulous meat and potato pies) and my father inherited those genes—he can whip up a mean chocolate cake at the drop of a hat.

My mother's side of the family is Scottish and Irish, and they have an unwritten rule that nobody should ever be allowed a cup of tea without also having a slice of cake (normally fruit or Madeira). When I was a child, my mother made sure the biscuit tin was always full of homemade goodies.

When I became a full-time mum and gave up my job as a textile designer, I found that I really missed having a creative outlet. I tried various crafty enterprises, but nothing fulfilled me. So I threw all my energy into my children's birthday parties, taking on board Julia Child's saying: "A party without cake is just a meeting." I channelled my creativity into making bigger and better birthday and celebration cakes, until I eventually reached the point when I began to think that my efforts might be good enough to sell commercially.

My first commercial cakes were mostly decorated with fondant models and cut-out flowers. I had no training in sugarcraft and knew that I couldn't (and therefore didn't want to) use piped decorations, as I was terrified the results would be bad, bordering on hideous. However, one of the very first cake commissions I received was for a 70th birthday cake, and the client wanted a "Happy Birthday Granddad" banner to go on the side. I was horrified, as I couldn't bear the thought of breaking out my piping bag. But working artists rarely have the chance to turn down a job from a client, particularly when their business is just starting out. So, I smiled and said, "Sure, no problem!"

It turned out that it was a problem. A massive problem. I can't remember actually crying, but after an hour spent piping, scraping off the results and then piping again, I'm sure the air turned a vivid shade of blue. I needed a different approach. I thought back to all the research I had done for my new career, and the many hours I had spent online looking at gorgeous cakes, and I recalled some cake decorators painting on fondant, adding features to sugar models. So I decided to do what the fifteen-year-old would-be dentist did: pick up a brush.

My mother knew it all along: I am happiest when I paint. As soon as I put the paintbrush, full of gloopy food colour, onto the fondant it was as if a cartoon lightbulb turned on above my head—it felt so much more natural than piping, and the text I had to paint flowed easily. If it felt this easy to write a message, I wondered what else I could paint. The next day I baked a batch of butterfly-shaped cookies, covered them with fondant and started painting flowers on them. And I've never looked back. There is now a permanent collection of jam jars lined up on my kitchen windowsill stuffed with paintbrushes, pots of food colour litter my work surfaces, we have cake coming out of our ears and, to this day, I'm still a terrible piper.

What started out as an escape from the housework, and a way to make a little extra money before eventually returning to textile design, has now become a career, and I couldn't be happier. I've been lucky enough to work for some amazing clients, on very exciting projects, and I get to travel the world teaching wonderfully enthusiastic sugarcraft students. Most of all, I love helping make people's special days even more special, and personal, for them.

With my training as an illustrator, I've always harboured ambitions to write and illustrate my own book. So you can imagine how thrilled I am to be able to write *The Painted Cake* for you. I hope that while reading this book you will be inspired to take up your own brush and paint, and that you will discover a totally new way of cake decorating. Remember, painting makes you happy!

FINDING YOUR PAINTING STYLE

Don't worry if you have no previous painting experience, either with fondant or in a more traditional medium—most of my students are absolute beginners, and they are all amazed at what can be achieved with a little direction and some practice. But it is important to be aware that when you paint on cake, the process is not like other cake-decorating practices where you learn the skills that enable you to create a carbon copy of a cake, every time. Painting is never like that, in any medium, and the results you get will vary slightly each time. As you work through each of the projects in this book, even though you will be decorating cakes (and the instructions, hints, and tips in this book are specifically about working on fondant), what you are really learning is how to paint. So, as well as being a cake decorator, you will also become an artist. I'm sure that you will find painting on fondant to be an incredibly personal, creative endeavour, and one that is extremely rewarding.

You may think that learning the technical skills to enable you to paint will be the hardest part of this process, but actually you will find that the projects provided will help you to demonstrate these skills relatively easily. No, the hardest lesson to learn when starting out as a painter is to love your own "hand"—this is an artist's term for the natural style that an individual paints in, and yours will always be unique. The term is very literal: it is your hand that works the paintbrush in a unique way, which leads to the creation of an individual style—and from that, unique works of art.

Learning to appreciate how your own "hand" looks is always difficult. In all my life as a designer, from art college onward, I have found there was always at least one fellow designer whose work I very much admired, but also felt a tinge of envy at their style. I often felt that my own work didn't come up to scratch. Now, when I teach a class, I find that most students have the same experience. They will be in awe of a fellow student's work and feel that their own work is inadequate. That little doubting voice should be ignored. It's important to always strive to get better but if, as you work through the projects in this book, you find that you are always comparing your painting to others, then your confidence will ebb away. Please, don't let that happen! Don't waste any time worrying that your work isn't good enough, because it is—it really is—you just need to learn to appreciate it. Accept that even though it is different from anybody else's, your own "hand," your own style of painting, is as good as anyone else's.

I tell you this because it's important to understand that painting is a personal pursuit. You will not be creating carbon copies of my work in the projects on these pages (unless you're a master forger, in which case I think you can probably make better money outside of the cake-decorating business). Some of you will discover that you have a much more delicate touch with a paintbrush, which will result in softer looking work. Some of you will have a more graphic style, or you may create a design that looks much more like a watercolour. Embrace your differences! At the end of teaching a class, I find it so exciting to see the variation in my students' work, even though they were all given the same design to work from. This is why I love painting so much—everyone's hand produces something a little different, something unique.

As you see your own style emerge while working through the projects in this book, please don't, on any account, try to fight it—or you will find your painting loses its integrity and you will feel dissatisfied with what you have created. Take plenty of time to practise, enjoy yourself, and above all else, let your inner artist out!

— Chapter 1 —

Your Kit

GETTING YOUR KIT TOGETHER

On the following pages, you will find an inventory of all the baking equipment and specialist decorating tools that you will need to make the projects in this book. You should be able to purchase the cake-making equipment from a general kitchen shop, or in the kitchen section of a large department store. If you are fortunate enough to have a cake-decorating supply shop near you, then you should be able to find the more specialised equipment there, or they will probably be able to order anything they don't have in stock. But, if you don't have access to a store, then you can find many specialist suppliers online—search for "cake-decorating equipment" or for the specific tool you need.

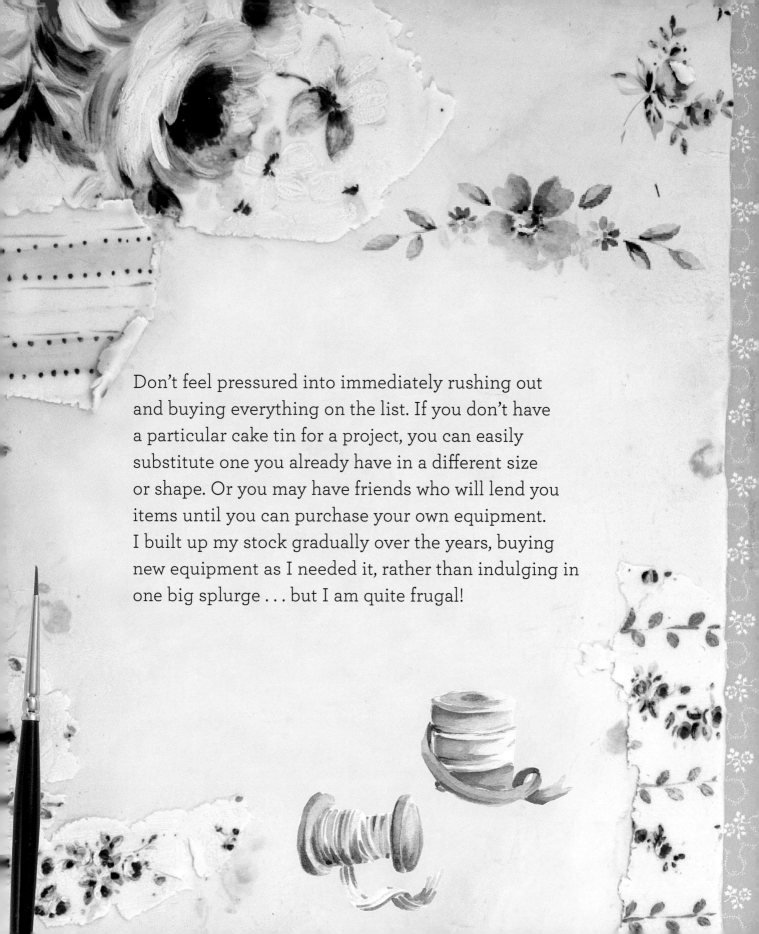

Don't feel pressured into immediately rushing out and buying everything on the list. If you don't have a particular cake tin for a project, you can easily substitute one you already have in a different size or shape. Or you may have friends who will lend you items until you can purchase your own equipment. I built up my stock gradually over the years, buying new equipment as I needed it, rather than indulging in one big splurge . . . but I am quite frugal!

BAKING EQUIPMENT

Cake tins—If you are just a beginner, then by all means use whatever cake tin you can get your hands on. However, if you wish to become a professional cake decorator, then I would advise you to invest in good-quality tins. The cake tins you buy from a specialist supplier will be made with a thicker metal (usually aluminium) which helps prevent any burning, and they will have perfect right angles and straight edges, both of which help when you cover and fill the cake. The sides of the tin should be at least 3"/75 mm high.

When making larger cakes that are assembled from separate layers, some bakers will use multiple tins of the same size to bake individual layers that are then put together to make the whole. The alternative is to bake the cake as a whole in a single tin and then cut it into layers afterwards. Tins can take up a lot of space and if you have multiples of the same size then you can't store them inside each other. Sadly, my kitchen is very tiny, with only one small cupboard for my tins, so this dictates how I bake: I stick to one tin per cake.

Most specialist cake-decorating supply shops sell cake tins measured in inches, however general kitchen shops are more likely to sell the tins in metric measurements, and sometimes these are not always the equivalent size in inches. If the size of your cake tin isn't exactly the same as the one I have used for a particular recipe, then you may find that the baking time is slightly affected, so just keep an eye on the cake as it comes to the end of its cooking time, to prevent any burning. Standard tin sizes are as follows:

> **Round tins:** 4"/100 mm; 5"/130 mm; 6"/150 mm; 7"/180 mm; 8"/200 mm; 9"/230 mm; 10"/250 mm
> **Square tins:** 4"/100 mm; 6"/150 mm; 8"/200 mm

Baking strips—These are insulating strips that go around your cake tin, to prevent the edges of the cake from burning and help your cake bake evenly. You can buy them from specialist baking suppliers.

Cupcake/muffin tins

Cupcake cases—I never use patterned cases when baking cupcakes; I find that the butter in the cakes affects the paper, and the pattern becomes lost. I bake the cupcakes in white or dark brown cases and then place the decorated cupcakes (still in their original wrappers) into my chosen cupcake cases. I bake the Fruit Cake recipe (page 55) in foil cases: these are thicker, which helps prevent the fruit burning while baking.

Baking trays—If you intend to make large batches of cookies you will need at least three baking trays. The same is true for cupcakes—buy three tins so that you can make up to 36 in each batch.

Cookie cutters

Cooling trays—Using stacked cooling trays is a fabulous way of saving space if you have a large order.

Baking (parchment) paper, for lining.

Greaseproof paper or tin foil, for wrapping fruit cakes.

Plastic wrap

A rubber spatula

A cake tester—If you don't have one, a skewer is perfectly adequate to check everything is baked through.

An oven thermometer—As every oven varies in its temperature range, you should double check your oven is at the right temperature for the recipe you are making. If the thermometer does not match the temperature you have set the oven at, then adjust the dial accordingly.

A sieve

A variety of bowls

A pastry brush—I find the brushes with natural bristles easiest to use, however I cannot find one that doesn't shed its hair—not so nice! I've resorted to using a pastry brush with silicone bristles; it's not as effective, but at least you don't end up with a mouthful of bristle while you eat your cake.

An electric hand-held whisk or a table-top mixer—You need an electric hand-held whisk for smaller cakes. For larger cakes, or to mix the ingredients for two cakes at the same time, I would advise you to invest in a table-top mixer, also known as a stand mixer.

Scales—I would always use electric scales, as they give a more accurate weight, but I know that some bakers prefer traditional scales; either type will be perfectly fine for the projects in this book.

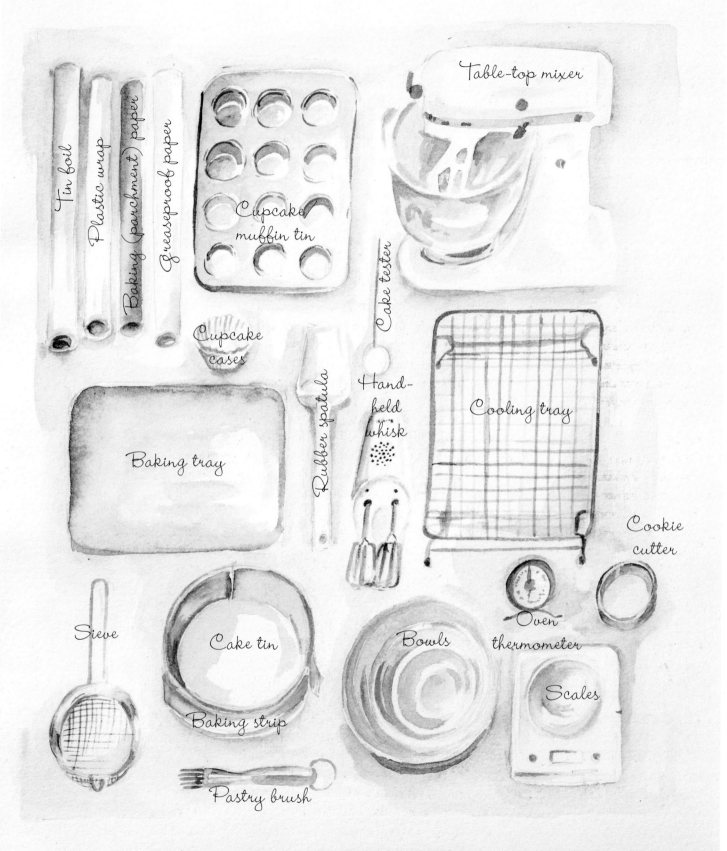

Tin foil

Plastic wrap

Baking (parchment) paper

Greaseproof paper

Cupcake/muffin tin

Table-top mixer

Cupcake cases

Cake tester

Hand-held whisk

Cooling tray

Rubber spatula

Baking tray

Cookie cutter

Sieve

Cake tin

Baking strip

Bowls

Oven thermometer

Scales

Pastry brush

CAKE-DECORATING EQUIPMENT

A cake leveller—You can just use a serrated knife, but I find this tool much easier.

An offset palette knife—This is sometimes called a crank-handle spatula, as the blade sits below the handle bent at an angle. This tool allows you to cover and smooth surfaces that you may not be able to reach with a conventional spatula.

A cake scraper—This is a flat rectangle of thin plastic or metal used to create perfectly straight sides of buttercream covering a cake, and I also use it to smooth down fondant.

Rolling pins—To roll out fondant, and cookie dough, you will need a long rolling pin about 18"/460 mm, preferably in plastic. Wooden rolling pins can leave marks and indentations on the fondant. You will find it useful to use a small rolling pin (6"/150 mm) when rolling out modelling paste.

Spacers—These are long, thin plastic strips that you use when you are rolling out fondant, marzipan, or cookie dough in order to get an even thickness. I use ¼"/5 mm spacers.

A turntable, tilted or untilted—Many of my students prefer the tilted turntable: if the cake is at an angle it is easier to paint the sides of the cake. I use an untilted turntable, which keeps the cake straight; I prefer this, especially when painting tiered cakes, because there is less chance of cracking or bulging sides.

Smoothers—These are paddles with handles that you use to create a beautiful smooth surface on the fondant. You place the flat surface of the smoother onto the surface of the fondant and, with even pressure, move it around the surface of the cake until it is perfectly smooth (or as near as you can get it).

Cake drums—These are cardboard boards thick enough to carry the weight of a cake (usually ½"/12 mm thick), even a tiered cake. The cardboard is covered with a foil coating, often silver or gold; there are also metallic pink or blue versions. However I always cover these boards with fondant and hide the edge with ribbon—my pet hate is an uncovered board under a beautiful cake.

Cake boards—Similar to cake drums, these are also made out of cardboard and are covered with foil, but they are much thinner than cake drums. You can buy ³⁄₁₆"/4 mm thick boards, double thick boards (⅛"/3 mm thick) or single thick boards (¹⁄₁₆"/2 mm thick). None of these boards would be suitable as the base board, as they are not thick enough to hold the weight of a cake. They are used to create support for tiered cakes.

Cocktail sticks

Dowels—Long thin poles used to add support to tiers, these can be plastic or wooden.

A small spirit level—This is a tool used to test whether a surface is completely horizontal. You may be able to find some cake-decorating suppliers that sell spirit levels, but your local DIY store will definitely stock them. Keep one purely for cake-decorating purposes.

A scalpel—Round-handled scalpels will be easier to use when cutting out fondant, but any scalpel is acceptable.

A foam mat—You place sugar-paste flowers or toppers on this mat while they dry out. They will dry out more quickly than on a work surface and will not stick.

An extruder—A large syringe or gun, this comes with a variety of discs which create different effects with fondant, such as rope, hair, or grass.

A ball tool—This modelling tool is a stick with a ball attached at each end. There are many uses for it, but for the designs in this book you'll use it to create ruffles.

A lace impression mat—This is a plastic or silicone mat that you press into rolled-out fondant which creates a lace pattern on the fondant surface. You can also buy lace impression rolling pins that you roll over the fondant to create the same effect.

A lace mould—This is a mould that you press thinly rolled modelling paste onto, to create a lace effect. You normally need to trim away any excess paste around the edge with a scalpel.

Cookie sticks

Edible-paint pen

A large star-tip piping nozzle—This is to create the lovely buttercream swirl on top of the cupcakes.

A piping (icing) bag—Plastic ones are disposable, or you can get cloth ones that can be washed and re-used.

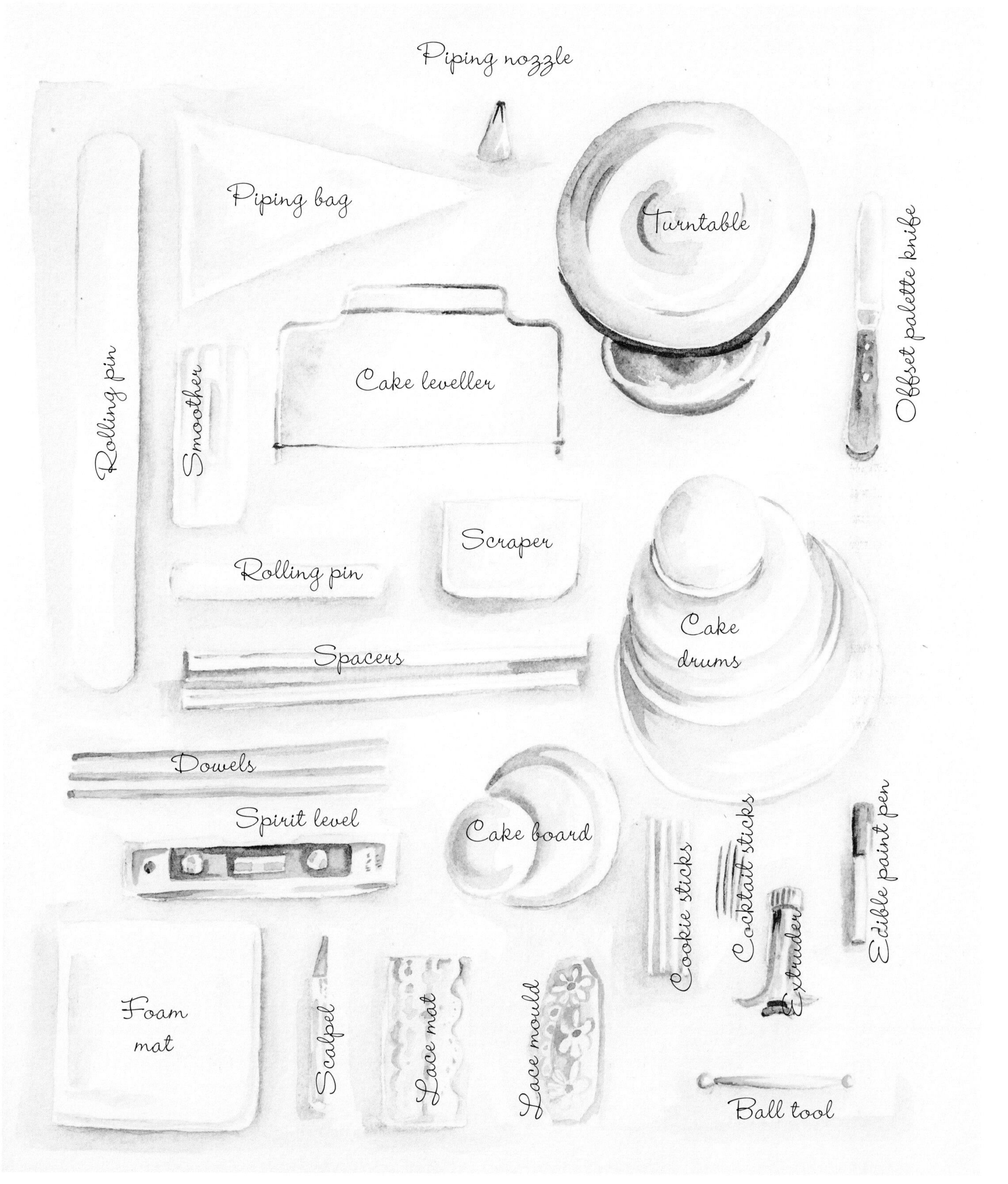

Piping nozzle

Piping bag

Turntable

Offset palette knife

Rolling pin

Smoother

Cake leveller

Scraper

Rolling pin

Cake drums

Spacers

Dowels

Spirit level

Cake board

Cookie sticks

Cocktail sticks

Edible paint pen

Extruder

Foam mat

Scalpel

Lace mat

Lace mould

Ball tool

PAINTING EQUIPMENT

A pot for water—You can also use a mug or clean jam jar.

An artist's palette—You can get these from most art and craft shops, however, when I started I used a plastic plate or the clean lid from a margarine tub—anything with a smooth plastic surface will work.

Paper towels

Paintbrushes, sizes 8, 4, and 0 round-tip brushes; a ¾"/20 mm flat brush—The bristles of a round-tip brush come to a point rather than having a square flat edge like a flat brush. While there are internationally recognised sizes for paintbrushes, there can be variation between manufacturers' distinction of each size.

For the purposes of these projects, a size 8 is a brush with a base width of ¼"/5 mm and is ¾"/20 mm long; a size 4 brush has a width of 1/16"/2 mm and a length of 5/8"/12 mm, and a size 0 brush has a width of 1/32"/1 mm and a length of 3/8"/7 mm. Don't worry if the brushes you use aren't exactly the same size as the measurements I have given—as long as they are roughly the sizes I have described, you will be able to paint all these projects. Some brushes may be the correct width but have a much longer length; I would steer clear of this type as long bristles can be hard to control.

If you have had any experience with traditional watercolour painting then you will know that a professional artist will normally use a sable-hair brush, as these are the best that you can buy. However, that's not the best for what we want to do; a brush made from natural hair combined with the gooey sugar paste and the sticky food colours will be unusable.

Instead, always buy synthetic brushes, with a round head. I normally opt for a medium price brush, but sometimes I "borrow" my children's cheap-as-chips paintbrushes and they are just as good. These three round-brush sizes (8, 4, 0) are all you will need to complete the painting part of the projects in this book and, unless you are painting a truly enormous cake, you will not need to buy a bigger brush.

The flat brush is used for moistening the fondant when you are applying edible printed icing, and also for creating the Splatter Cake (page 209).

As with all the equipment mentioned here, you should keep your brushes solely for cake-decorating purposes.

Gold edible spray—You can buy this spray from specialist cake-decorating suppliers. It looks like something a graffiti artist would use, but it is totally edible (it should state this on the tin, otherwise you have bought the wrong product!).

Edible food colours—The massive growth in the baking and cake-decorating industry has brought many fabulous products to the marketplace and there is a very wide variety of food colours that are suitable for painting onto fondant. I use paste colours because they have an opaque quality. You can use gels, but they will be more translucent (this will result in a different quality to your work, and in the long run you may discover this suits your hand better); but some varieties will not dry out on the fondant and remain tacky.

You can also use lustre dusts and liquid colours, and again each different type of colouring will give different results. A word of caution: there are powder and lustre dusts available from cake-decorating suppliers that are not actually edible (I know, this sounds counter-intuitive). Cake decorators dust these products on to sugar-paste flowers that, even though they may be placed onto a cake, are not for consumption. If you are using a powdered product, please make sure that it is an edible variety.

Gold paint—There are lots of types available. Find a liquid one that can be diluted in water. Some require alcohol to paint with. You can use gold lustre dust, but it tends to revert to a powder once it has dried and so can be smudged very easily.

White powder—Often overlooked, one of the most important colours in your paintbox is white. Again, make sure that it is edible. I always use the powdered version rather than liquid, as I tend to find the latter is too translucent to paint with. If you can't get hold of white powder, then try a very pale lustre dust, which will give you the same results. Mixing up the white into a paste for your painting is a skill that takes a bit of practice: if it's too watery, you won't see it on the

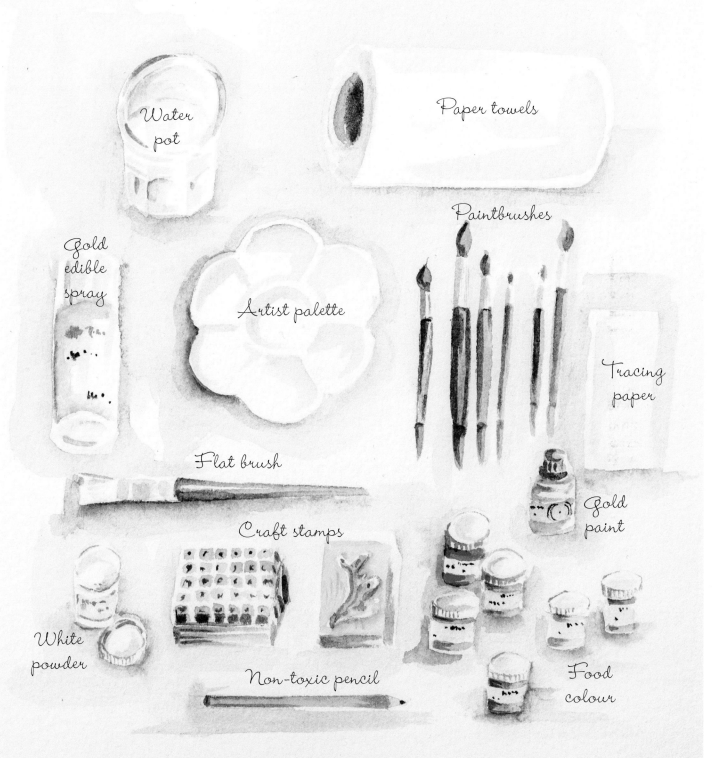

Water
pot

Paper towels

Paintbrushes

Gold
edible
spray

Artist palette

Tracing
paper

Flat brush

Gold
paint

Craft stamps

White
powder

Non-toxic pencil

Food
colour

fondant, but if it's too thick it will crack when it dries. Once you have applied the white you need to either work another colour into it immediately or leave it to dry completely. This is because, as the white dries, it forms a skin, and if you paint on top of it at this point in the drying process then you will just lift the skin up (the same is true for the metallic colours).

You also need to be sparing with the white, and just use it for little touches in minimal areas. It will bleach through any colour painted on top or underneath it, and can have the effect of deadening the design if you use too much of it. Frequently, if my students feel that they do not have enough tonal value in a flower they have painted, they go a little bit crazy with the white in an attempt to rectify it, but this only results in their design becoming terribly flat.

A note of caution: if you paint on top of dark-coloured fondant with white (or, indeed, any other colour) the background colour will bleed through, and sometimes colours you were not expecting will appear. I once painted white onto grey fondant, and the flowers I was designing became blue! So, if you have plans to create a design on coloured fondant, then have a practice run beforehand to be completely sure that the colour palette you have chosen will work.

Non-toxic pencils—Most pencils that you buy from art and craft shops are made from graphite and are non-toxic, but double-check the make-up of any pencil that you intend to use on a design.

Tracing paper—You can purchase this from an art supply shop, or you can use greaseproof paper.

Craft stamps—You can purchase these from art supply shops. Make sure you keep them solely for cake-decorating use.

Yellow
Orange
Red
Pink
Dark pink
Purple
Blue
Bright green

Soft green
Dark green
Brown
Black
Grey
White
Gold

Edible food colour chart

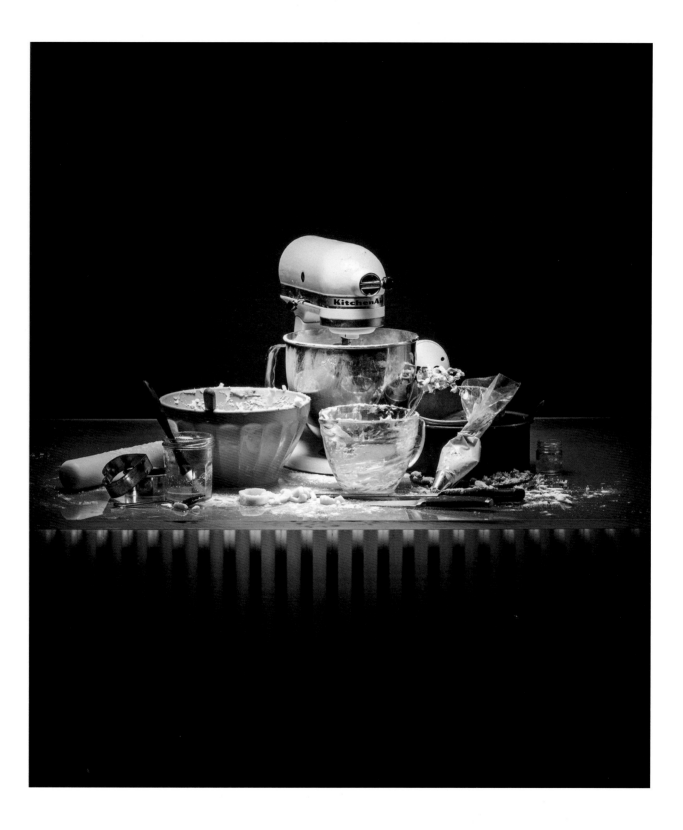

Chapter 2

Design and Painting Techniques

GETTING STARTED

In this chapter, I will take you through general
techniques and practices for painting on fondant.
I describe a few different methods for transferring the
designs. Once you are confident in your skills, I would
encourage you to paint using the freehand method,
as this helps to create a looser, more expressionistic
feel—but you should use the method that will make
the process easier for yourself. My motto is use any
technique if the result is worth it (that's only related
to painting, of course—not in my private life, although
there was that one time . . .).

Here I teach you how to water down your paint so it is the right consistency. You will also learn how to mix tones—one of the most important skills to master—and how to add interest to a design with highlights and lowlights. Your paintbrushes are your most important tools and I give you advice on how to care for them properly, so you get the most use from them (otherwise you may need to change brushes after just one project). These are all skills you will need to use in the various projects. You will find that more specific methods and details are included in each project, but do read the following notes thoroughly so you have a good understanding of the techniques. Until you feel very comfortable with these practices, keep referring back to this chapter.

It is best to use the lightest tone of brown

Positioning guidelines on cake

CREATING YOUR BASIC LAYOUT

Before beginning to paint a design onto a cake, I sketch very faint circles to indicate where any flowers (or other elements) of the design will be placed. I find it difficult to begin painting onto a completely blank canvas—somehow my mind functions much better if there is already a mark on the fondant. I have often observed that my students sometimes take more than ten minutes to make their first mark on the fondant—they sit looking at their brush, then at their cake and then back again, as an anguished look flits across their face. I appreciate how daunting it can be because I still feel nervous every time I approach a new design. But this is all part of the excitement when painting onto fondant. So, by creating a rough outline, you have, in effect, already sullied your pristine canvas, and any marks you now make will only improve it. Well, that's my logic, anyway.

The second reason is much more practical, which is that you need to create a rough layout before you commit to a design. You don't want to begin work on your cake's final group of flowers only to discover that you have left too much of a gap between that cluster and its neighbour. Worse, you don't want to realise that there is not enough space left between the flowers you've already painted to add the final elements without everything becoming too crowded.

So, you should always create a rough layout first—but even taking this advice into account, be prepared for things to change as you go along with the design. Painting is a fluid process, and the spacing between design groups will slightly alter as you build up all the various elements of the design. Even so, the difference in spacing will be a lot less pronounced if you do use a rough guide.

You can paint your guideline in any colour, but think about how this will affect the final design. I nearly always paint my guidelines in a very watered-down brown. Experience has told me that this will blend with most of the colours I use. Using a pink guideline will look great for the flowers, but it will clash terribly with the green of the leaves, creating a muddy colour. The faint brown I use mixes in with the other colours and simply adds tone, rather than clashes with my palette.

When you are painting flowers which have larger petals, such as roses, you shouldn't need to wash out the guidelines—just paint over them. However, with smaller flowers (such as forget-me-nots) or flowers which have many small petals (like daisies), you should wash out the lines before you paint. This is because the faint brown outline can appear in the gaps between the elements, spoiling the overall appearance of the design.

A non-toxic pencil outline

A painted outline

Transferring a design to the fondant

TRANSFERRING A DESIGN TO A CAKE

Although I will always mark out a rough outline of where the key elements will appear in my designs, this is not definitive and will only show positioning guidelines. I usually paint flowers or leaves "freehand"—this is the term for painting without a comprehensive outline of the subject, letting the final appearance be guided by the flow of my hand. So, if I am painting a rose on a cake, I may paint a circle (as described opposite) so that I know where to place the rose, but that will be the only guideline I employ. Everything else will be painted freehand: I use my brush to create the petals, rather than painting an outline of a flower first and then "colouring in." By working freehand, I can achieve a design which has a much more lively quality with more movement and personality in the finished piece.

That said, I do appreciate that if you are a beginner, you might find the thought of freehand painting very intimidating. If the idea of using a more detailed, planned guideline appeals to you, then go for it. As I say to my students, you must find the easiest method that allows you to paint, so maybe drawing the outline of a flower first will give you more confidence. It is better to paint using this process than not to paint at all.

You can paint the shape of the flower and its petals with watered-down brown paint, or you can use a non-toxic pencil. If at first you feel that drawing a flower (or any other element) is too difficult, you can trace a design onto the fondant. I often use this method if I am going to be painting a figure or an animal—tracing will make sure that the element will fit on the cake, and that the proportions are correct.

To make a tracing, lay a piece of tracing paper over the design you wish to copy, and mark the outline with a non-toxic pencil. Then turn the tracing paper over and, on the reverse of the sheet, trace over the outline you have just made. You need to make quite dark marks on this second side, as these are the lines that will actually be transferred onto the fondant. Then turn the paper over again to the original side and carefully lay it on the fondant. Use your pencil to once again press over the lines of the design. After you have retraced a small amount, check that the design is transferring to the fondant. If not, try again, pressing a little harder with the pencil. If the marks still don't appear, then you need to take the paper off the fondant, make darker pencil lines on the reverse side of the paper, and then try again. When you are tracing your design onto the cake, be very careful not to lean on the fondant or press too hard with the pencil, as you will create bumps in the surface.

Too much liquid, too shiny

Colours bleeding

Colours dripping and running

USE WATER INSTEAD OF ALCOHOL

Most cake decorators who paint on fondant will advise you to use a clear alcohol, such as vodka, to water down your paint. People often assume that this is to prevent any contamination by germs, but it's actually because the alcohol will evaporate more quickly and therefore the fondant will not become soggy. However, if you are planning on doing a lot of painting, you will find that you can easily use up a bottle of vodka in just a few cakes (not because it's a stressful pastime). So, in an effort to keep my costs down, I started using boiled water, and if you can master my technique, it is just as good and a lot cheaper. The trick is to use your brush with as little liquid trapped in its bristles as you can get away with—you must constantly dab off any excess fluid onto paper towels, or scrape excess water off your brush onto the lip of your water pot.

I always have one or two students in each class who seem to find it impossible to paint in this "dry" manner (referring back to everyone having their own "hand," these students have a particularly wet method of painting). If you do prefer this technique, then by all means try using alcohol to water down your colours.

USING TOO MUCH LIQUID

The tell-tale signs indicating that you have used too much liquid when watering down your paints are as follows:

- Any paint on the surface of the cake will look excessively shiny and will tend to form blobs, rather than the clean brushstrokes needed.
- Colours will begin to bleed into each other. You will find it difficult to create tonal differences, because the paint is so wet that any darker tone you paint on top of the lighter tone simply gets watered down.
- When you try to paint darker tones onto your design, you lift off any previously applied colour because the fondant underneath has become too soggy to absorb the paint.
- Colours drip and run down the side of the cake. It takes longer than 10 minutes for any paint on the cake to become totally dry or to feel slightly tacky to the touch.
- When you have finished painting and it has dried, gently run your fingers over the surface—it should feel flat to the touch. Depressions or "craters" under the painted colours indicate that you have used too much liquid, causing the fondant to melt. You can't really fix this, so try and use less water on your next attempt.

Mixing tones

A colour wheel

MIXING AND USING TONES

To create the effect of light and shade in any design, you must lay down the paint in layers of colours and tones. The lightest colour or tone is always the first layer to be painted, and then darker colours and tones are added on top.

In order to perfect the painting technique described in this book, it is important that you create the lighter tones of a particular colour by watering down the paint, rather than adding white powder (as already mentioned, using too much white paint will result in a flat, toneless design).

Let each layer of tone dry before you paint the next layer on top of it. Otherwise the two layers will start to mix together and you will lose the definition between the tones.

HOW TO MIX A TONE

1   Dip a damp paintbrush into the pot of your chosen colour, then wipe the bristles onto the palette to transfer the paint.
2   Wash all the colour out of your brush. You do this by knocking it from side-to-side in the pot of water—don't push the brush around on the bottom of the pot, as this will ruin the bristles.
3   With the brush now full of clean water, scrape the bristles onto a clean area of the palette. This should leave you with a small pool of water on your palette.
4   With your brush, pick up some of the neat colour you previously transferred to the palette and then add it to the pool of water.
5   Repeat as required, adding colour to the water until you have created the tone you need.
6   Using this method, it should be simple to gently build up any of the tones that you will need. Don't try it the other way round (adding water to the colour), as you will find it impossible to create any light tones.
7   As you work through the projects in this book, you will need to create at least three different tones of each colour used to create each design's elements. With very pale colours (such as yellow), this will not be possible, but you can get around this problem by using a "harmonious" colour as a darker tone. Harmonious colours are found next to each other on the colour wheel, so if you want to paint a yellow flower you can use orange or even pink to create the lovely depth of tone you need to make an attractive design. If you are painting yellow leaves, then you can use green as a darker tone, as this is also a harmonious colour of yellow.

Adding highlights

Adding lowlights

Leave unpainted areas

HIGHLIGHTS AND LOWLIGHTS

If you are a complete beginner to painting, then I imagine your last experience of producing any artwork would have been during your schooldays. I would also lay a bet that at some point during these art lessons you were given a project (using charcoal and white chalk) to teach you the theory of directional light. Maybe you had to draw a sphere, a box and possibly a triangle, all of which were placed under a very strong light. One side of these objects would be white where the light was hitting it, and the side in shadow would have been black. Your teacher would have emphasised that in every future painting or drawing you must consider the effect of light on the subject. While this is certainly true (I don't want to make art teachers angry), in reality there are many different light sources hitting an object. So when you are working through the projects in this book, please do not imagine your bunch of flowers is sitting under one bright light. This is not to say you shouldn't introduce highlights and shading into your designs—you definitely should. If you don't, the resulting design would be flat and uninteresting. So, consider the light sources that will give your design a more natural feel.

In most of the projects, I indicate that you should "add highlights to the leaves and flowers." Usually, these parts are painted with white to represent areas that reflect sunlight. But remember that the light source will come from many different directions, so don't add the highlights to the same side of every leaf or flower.

If on the other hand I instruct you to add "lowlights" or shading to a particular design element, this is to represent an area that is in shadow. If a leaf has been painted so that it appears to be partly behind another leaf or flower, then the area where the overlap occurs will be the darkest part of the leaf. Use this same theory where petals overlap, and remember that often the area of the petal nearest to the centre of the flower will be in shadow too.

LEAVE UNPAINTED AREAS

Rather than completely filling in elements of your design (like a "paint-by-numbers" puzzle, where every section must be filled with colour), try and leave some areas within each design that are free of colour. The area left free of paint will (naturally) be the base colour of the fondant, normally white.

There are a couple of different reasons why you should do this. First, the unpainted area of base fondant acts as your very lightest tone, it represents the area of a flower or a leaf that is reflecting the most light, and so there will be more of a contrast with the darker tones. This results in a flower with more depth and a more realistic feel—and essentially you get your lightest highlight tone for free.

Secondly, if you meticulously paint in every last millimetre of a flower, you leave nothing to the imagination; you are presenting your audience with the representation of your perception of what that flower is. Now, if you have painted a perfect flower, then there is no problem, but unfortunately most people (myself very much included) will not be able to reach this level of artistry. If you leave unpainted areas on a flower, the viewers will subconsciously use their imagination to fill in the gaps and the design will appear more perfect to their eyes than it is in reality. Essentially, less is more: your designs will tend to look better if you don't overpaint them.

DRYING TIMES

If you have been painting without using too much liquid, you will find that each layer of colour will not take longer than ten minutes to dry (if your painting is taking much longer than this, then you have probably prepared your colours with too much water). Remember, dab off as much liquid from your brush as you can onto a sheet of paper towels before you start painting, so that you are using a drier stroke, which is more suitable for the technique used in these projects.

When I am painting groups of flowers over a cake, I will normally finish just the first cluster before moving on—I won't add the initial colour layer for multiple flowers, but only focus on the first bunch in the design. Once I feel that these flowers are as perfect as I can make them, and I have an idea in my head how each bloom will be built up, then I will paint the rest of the flowers stage by stage. After seeing how this first flower cluster looks, I will then be more comfortable painting the initial pale tone of all the remaining flowers and leaves, and be happy to build up the other layers one by one across the whole design. This helps to ensure that (excluding that first group) each layer of colour has dried before I paint any darker tones for the rest of the design.

Because the final layer of colour is the darkest, and thus the least diluted, it is usually neat colour paste and this will take much longer to completely dry—with this in mind, I always leave any painted cakes or cookies to dry overnight. But sometimes (even after this time) areas painted with the neat colour can still feel tacky to the touch. As I only ever use a small amount of strong colour on my designs (including all the projects in this book), I have never found this to be an issue with cakes or cupcakes. It can, however, be

Packaged cookies

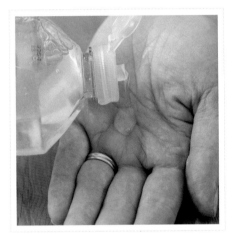
Use a small amount of liquid dish soap

Gently pull the bristles into a point

problematic with cookies that you plan to package in cellophane bags because any wet or tacky paint can smudge and transfer paint to the wrapper. To avoid this, before packing the cookies, use some paper towels to dab off the excess colour, then gently ease the cookie into the cellophane bag, keeping the painted side away from the surface of the bag. Make sure the cookie is as far into the bag as it can go, and secure the package with a ribbon. Once fastened like this, the cookie should not be able to jiggle about within the packaging and you should be smudge-free.

USE THE CORRECT PAINTBRUSH

As I mentioned in the previous chapter, for all the painting projects you will only need to use the three brush sizes I have recommended: 8, 4, and 0. You will notice as you work through the various projects in *The Painted Cake* that I will advise you which size paintbrush to use for different areas of the designs. It is always best to use a larger paintbrush rather than a smaller one, because you will find it easier to create the marks that make a more beautiful work of art. If you use a brush that is too small, your painting will look overworked and scratchy. When I'm working on a large multi-tiered cake, I use a size 8 brush, even for very fine details. If, when you come to paint any small features (such as stalks or small dots), you find that your marks look heavy, then by all means switch to a smaller brush at that point (just make sure to return to a larger brush when you start to paint the bigger features again).

CARE FOR YOUR PAINTBRUSHES

The medium you are working with is basically just sugar and therefore it can make the bristles of your brushes very sticky. This stickiness soon causes the bristles to splay and they can quickly lose their shape (a good reason not to spend too much money on your brushes). You can prolong the life of your brush very simply: after you have finished painting, wash your brushes in clean cold water (don't use hot water as this can destroy the bristles), then pour a small amount of liquid dish soap onto your palm, and gently rub the bristles in the soap in a circular motion—don't jab. Then, with the tips of your fingers, pull the brush back into a point. Finally, leave the brush standing with the tip pointing upwards in a pot to dry—ideally leave it at least overnight before you use it again. When you are ready to start painting again, gently wash the soap out of the bristles; you should find that the brush has returned to its original shape.

Keep your hand still

KEEP YOUR HAND STILL

Believe it or not, although I paint for a living, my hands are actually quite shaky—I can't hold a teacup and saucer without the sound of intense rattling. But through practice, I have learnt to control this shakiness when I paint. If I am painting a single-tiered cake, I will first place the cake straight down on a table to paint the top. While I paint I sit on a chair (rather than stand) and I lean my elbow on the table to give my painting hand stability. When it comes to painting the side of a cake, I will put the cake onto a turntable and, again, I will lean my elbow on the table. Frequently I find that the side of my palm touches the cake—this is pretty much unavoidable—but I make sure that it is not pressing into it, as this would create dents in the fondant. If I feel that I am at risk of leaning too hard on the fondant, I will hold my painting wrist with my other hand, and this then keeps my painting hand steady. If you find you are still struggling while painting onto the side of the cake, you may find it easier to use a tilted turntable which will hold your cake at an angle more suitable for painting.

When I am painting cakes with multiple tiers, I normally find that I need to stand up in order to paint the top of the uppermost tier. This can be quite tricky because with the tallest cakes the table is way below your painting surface and so there is nothing to lean your arm on. Again, for stability you can hold the wrist of your painting hand with the opposite one. Whatever method you use, make sure you keep checking that you are not denting the fondant.

Painting flowers and leaves

As you work through the projects in this book, I give you specific instructions for creating the flowers and leaves in particular designs. However, there are some general rules to follow that will help you when you are painting the cakes.

USE A REFERENCE

I very rarely paint anything without using a reference. This is because it is easy for your brain to play tricks on you. You may think that you know what a rose looks like, but if you try to paint one from memory, the result will be a slightly odd looking flower. I have many files and folders cluttering my office, all full of torn-out pages from magazines, old birthday cards or scraps of fabric, and I use these all the time as references for my designs.

As you work through the projects in this book, you will see step-by-step pictures, showing you how to paint the elements of each design. I create similar worksheets for the classes I teach, which my students can use during the lesson. I have noticed that most of them never look at this reference, and if they do, it is just a quick cursory glance. This is not the right way to use a reference. My rule of thumb is that if you are painting for five minutes, spend at least half of that time studying the reference. This is so that you have time to really study it and you will be painting what you see, rather than what you think you see.

Once you have confidence in your painting skills, you may wish to create your own design. Find some references for the flowers you wish to paint and work from these. It is a sad but true fact that a painted design is never as beautiful as the reference it has been taken from (I'm speaking for myself here too), so if you choose a picture of an ugly or strange-looking flower, odds are your painting will be even more ugly and strange. Pick your references with care—choose beautiful pictures of gorgeous flowers, or even pick up a bunch from your local florist and paint those—and your design will be fabulous.

PERFECTING PETALS

Use your brush to create the petals. This may seem obvious, but I often observe many of my students using small, indecisive brush marks, or painting an outline which they then "fill in." The freer your mark-making, the more pleasing to the eye your painting will be. When you are painting larger flowers, use your whole arm to make the movement; for all sizes of designs keep plenty of rotation in your wrist. Stop every so often to make sure you are not hunching your shoulders, because this can give your painting a tighter feel (and, in this case, tight is not good). Try to use a maximum of three brushstrokes for each layer of colour on a petal; any more and the flower will start to look overworked.

Make every petal on a flower look slightly different. A real flower will never have petals that are uniformly the same. The gap in between these petals will also vary—some will have a larger gap whereas others will overlap. If you paint every petal in the same manner, with the same-sized gap between them, you will end up with a very stylised, stiff-looking flower.

KEEPING THE FLOWER SIZE CONSISTENT

If you are covering a cake with painted flowers, the size of those flowers may need to be consistent. As you paint each flower, measure it with your paintbrush or your fingers, and compare its size to the first flower you painted, to help ensure consistency. Alternatively, if you wish, you can make a small template the size of your flower and keep comparing your flowers to it to make sure that you are not increasing or decreasing in size. To do this, cut a circle of paper to match the size of your first flower and use this as your reference.

FLOWERS FROM ALL SIDES

To add more variation in a design, you should paint flowers from different angles. So one may be painted as if you are looking straight down at the head of the flower, one could be from a side angle (so you wouldn't be able to see the centre of that flower), and you should include variations in between. Also, remember to paint the buds and semi-open buds of a particular flower to add more interest.

SIDE-ON ROSES

1   When you start painting a rose, begin with the top petals, the middle one of which should be the highest point of the flower. The petals in the middle should be painted with a downward stroke, but the petals on either side of these should bend inwards. As you make the brushstroke, put more pressure on the bristles at the beginning of the mark and gradually release the pressure and lift the brush off the fondant towards the end of the stroke. I call this technique 'feathering', and painting in this manner creates a softer mark with lots of movement, resulting in a more natural finish to the flower.

2   After you have finished painting the middle of the rose, paint the side petals. These are larger than the top petals and sweep across the front of the rose—the centre of these petals will be thicker than the tips. You must be careful not to create a strong line
of petals, so make sure that they cross over each other, and don't forget to leave some unpainted areas to represent highlights.

3   When I am teaching classes, the majority of my students tend to finish their roses at this point. This results in squashed looking flowers, because they have forgotten to add in the bottom petals. The bottom petals are two or three very large petals, which you can make with one or two brush marks each.

4   You will now have created the shape of a beautiful rose in a light base tone. The next step is to add the centre with a darker tone. The mistake most people make is to paint the centre too high up or too far down. The bottom of the centre should be right at the middle point of the flower, and then the rest of the centre is painted in marks moving up from this point. Any petals you paint in the centre should mirror the shape of the first layer of petals that you have painted.

5   As you add the layers of tones onto the rose, make sure that you don't paint directly over the marks you have already made: make your new marks at a slightly different angle, or change the size or slightly offset them. Each mark will look like a petal, so the more marks you make the more petals the rose will appear to have.

STRAIGHT-ON ROSES

1   This rose is painted to give the appearance that you are looking straight down onto its centre. The shape of this type of rose is very circular—however, it should still have distinctive petal shapes around the edge.

2   One of the issues my students often find with this type of rose is creating the centre. They tend to paint rings of colour rather than a darker centre which gradually becomes lighter.

SIDE-ON ROSES

Top petals

Feathering technique

Side petals

Bottom petals

Centre petals too high

Tones

STRAIGHT-ON ROSES

Outside petals

Incorrectly painted with uniform rings

Correctly painted

ROSEBUDS

Too small

Too large

Just right

FLOWERS AND LEAVES

Different-shaped petals

Keep petal sizes consistent

Daisies with correct spacing

Daisies with spacing too uniform

Painting centres of open-faced flowers

Painting leaves correctly

ROSEBUDS

1   When you are painting rosebuds, remember to keep their size consistent with the open rose. They shouldn't be too big or too small. (And, yes, I am just like Goldilocks.)

FLOWERS WITH FIVE PETALS

1   These are flowers such as forget-me-nots, cherry blossoms, bluebells, or even just small generic filler flowers. You must consider the shape of the petal: is it round or pointed or heart-shaped? Even though you do need to create some slight differences between each petal on a particular flower, they still must be fairly consistent in shape—you shouldn't paint a cherry blossom flower with four very round petals and one very pointy petal, they would be better as four round petals and one slightly pointy.

2   The other big mistake people make with this type of flower is keeping sizes consistent. All of the flowers in a bunch of forget-me-nots will be much the same size; there shouldn't be one flower that is twice the size of the others. So as you paint them keep referring back to the first flowers you painted and check the sizes.

DAISY OR CHRYSANTHEMUM TYPES

1   These are flowers which are open-faced and are made up of many long thin petals. Use no more than three strokes to create the petals of these flowers, and for small daisies just one or two. Start your stroke at the outer tip of the petal and move the brush towards the centre of the flowers using the feathering technique (see "side-on roses," page 38). Make sure that each petal has a slightly different shape and that the gap between each varies.

2   When you paint the middle of these flowers, do not add the detail and shading in a complete circle around the edge of the centre. Choose one area where you will add more detail and leave some areas unpainted.

3   The method I have described above is the natural way that I paint this type of flower; however, many of my students prefer to paint the centre first and then the petals. If you find this a more natural way to paint this type of flower, then by all means go for it.

PAINTING LEAVES

Speaking personally, I feel a design only truly comes alive once I have added the leaves. Does this make me sound like some kind of crazy leaf-lady? Possibly I am. Don't focus on the flowers—even though they are naturally the highlight of the design—to the detriment of the leaves and stalks that hold them. The addition of leaves can create movement and add interest to a design, and they can also pull other elements in a group together to produce more consistency throughout a pattern. The most important rule to remember when painting leaves is to always paint in the direction of the veins. Most leaves have a central vein that runs through the middle of the leaf and smaller veins branching off, so any mark that you make while painting a leaf must reflect this. However do not try to recreate a botanical drawing where every single vein and shadow on the leaf is represented. You can paint a leaf with just one or two brushstrokes, but even these marks should imitate the veins. Do not paint any lines that run in an opposite direction to the natural veins on a leaf.

Always make sure the shape of any leaf you paint is accurate to the flower you are painting—you will be surprised how often an incorrect leaf subconsciously jars with the viewer. For example, if you are painting a rose leaf, it needs to have a slightly serrated edge; a daisy leaf is long and thin, and hydrangea leaves are round and fat.

Painting the side of a cake

Many of the projects in this book feature designs that cover the whole of the cake—that is, not just the top but the side too. When you are working on these designs, you will need to be especially aware of issues that can arise when painting designs that spill over onto the side of the cake.

The design flows . . .

. . . all around the side . . .

. . . and top of the cake.

Most flowers are actually quite circular in shape—think of a daisy or a chrysanthemum. But if you paint a true, accurate circle that spreads over an edge and then take a good look at it, it will seem really squashed even though technically it is perfectly round—it's an optical illusion caused by the shape being interrupted by the angle of the edge. You will need to consider this effect as you paint and try to work around it. You should elongate the circular shape of the flower slightly, both across the top and down the side of the cake, until it looks correct to the eye (even though it will now be an oval). If you trace your flowers onto a cake, just be aware of this issue, and be prepared to change the flowers slightly from the original tracing when you start to paint them.

Another common problem I have seen my students struggle with when adding flowers onto the side of their cake is that they find it difficult to continue to paint the design elements in various orientations. They end up painting everything climbing vertically from the base. Although this may be true in life, when you are painting onto a cake you need to show the flowers or stalks running in more than just one direction, or your design will look too artificial. The side of your cake should include at least a couple of blooms that are pointing down. Most can still be in an upward direction, but you must then take care to angle them slightly.

Don't just paint complete groups of flowers on the side of the cake—or even paint only entire flowers. It is also desirable—actually, I would say necessary—to include small fragments of the flowers, such as the tip of some petals or a stalk with just a few leaves. This will then give the impression that the design would have carried on beyond the boundary of the fondant rather than simply finishing at the end of the cake.

In fact, I advise you to not leave an unpainted gap around the bottom of the cake, but paint right to the edge. If you accidentally make marks on the covered cake board you can easily wash these away once you have finished, or you could even paint your cake and then transfer it to a clean board.

Troubleshooting

The process that always impresses my students
the most is the ease with which you can erase marks
on the fondant. They are delighted to learn that any
mistakes they make don't have to be there forever
(or until some kind person comes along and eats
the evidence).

Dab water on the affected area

Dry your brush well

Lift the colour off

HOW TO FIX MISTAKES

It's really important to understand that mistakes are a perfectly normal part of the process: at some point in every project you'll make a slip, or be unhappy with the shape or colour of an element. And that's fine. There really are no mistakes you can't rectify, even if your last resort is to scrub things out and start again. When I was a student, one of the exercises that seemed to be a favourite of my tutor was to take a piece of work that you were unhappy with, tear it up and then use it to make a collage. Obviously this would be impossible with a fondant-covered cake; however, the principle can be the same—mistakes are just pathways to a new ending. I always make mistakes (contrary to what I tell my husband), so it's crucial that I have a thorough, failsafe method for rectifying my errors and putting things straight.

1   Fill your paintbrush with clean water—make sure no colour remains in your brush. You may find it easier to use a size 8 brush rather than a smaller one.

2   Gently dab the water over the area you wish to remove. Be aware of any drips running down the side of the cake—you may find it handy to have some paper towels ready for any eventuality.

3   Clean your brush and dry it on paper towels. Use the clean, dry brush to pick up the watery colour on your painting. Then wash all the colour out of the brush and dry it again.

4   Keep repeating the steps above until the element you wish to remove has disappeared. Then gently wipe over the wet section with paper towels. Be very careful not to smudge any of the painting you have not removed while you do this.

5   If you can still see any colour left, then repeat the process. Once the area has dried completely, there should not be a mark.

6   Sometimes there may be a slight watermark remaining on the fondant after the area has dried. I normally leave this, as usually once you have finished painting you cannot see it. However, if you are left with a mark that you are unhappy about, then you can take a small piece of fondant (the same colour as your base) and rub it over the area, and you should find the watermark will

Once dry, there should be no mark

Use a scalpel to shave off marked fondant

disappear. Alternatively, when the painting has been completed, rub a small amount of cornflour (cornstarch) into the mark, and it should vanish.

7   You can erase mistakes in this way even a few days after painting, although if you leave it too long you may have to work a little harder to get all of the colour out.

8   If there is a small amount of cracking in your fondant base, you will sometimes find it difficult to remove the colour, as it can seep into the cracks. If this happens, simply follow the steps above to remove the majority of the colour, then carefully use a scalpel to shave any remaining colour off the fondant.

HOW TO FIX DESIGN PROBLEMS

When I am teaching, a student may ask me what is wrong with their design. Often there is nothing wrong—they are just lacking confidence in their own hand. However, sometimes there may be a slight issue and, although the student can tell something is not right, they do not know what it is.

If you have a nagging doubt about your finished piece, but just can't put your finger on the problem, here are a few methods to use for troubleshooting:

1   Check through the various issues discussed in this chapter. Are all the flowers of an equal size, are the bunches evenly spaced, have you created depth of tone in your design, have you used the correct sized paintbrush, or does your painting look scratchy? How closely does your painting correspond to the reference you used, have you spent enough time studying the reference, or did you paint the design from memory?

2   Step away from the cake (move on, nothing to see here). Just give yourself a 15-minute break—make a cup of tea, read a magazine, or follow my example and look at some pretty cakes on the internet. When you come back to your design, you should be able to look at it with fresh eyes and you may be able to discover the problem.

3   Hold the cake in front of a mirror—looking at the reflection of your design rather than at the design itself can help to stop your brain thinking too hard and give it a chance to work out what the problem is. (Do be careful not to lose your grip and drop it!)

4   Get a second opinion. If you have someone nearby you can call on, get them to have a look at the cake, or send a picture of the cake to a friend who you can trust to give you an honest opinion (someone with an artistic background would be perfect). They may be able to put your mind at rest and declare that it is "perfect," or they may pinpoint any problems that need to be looked at.

5   Think about the angle of your body while you are painting. If you are sitting at a slant towards your cake, this may affect the way that you paint. Try and sit as straight as you can, facing the cake.

6   Visit an optometrist and have your eyes checked. You may think that I'm joking, but in fact I am serious. I have an astigmatism in one eye and I tend to draw and paint objects with a slight lean to the right. Because I am aware of this, I know that I have to compensate and so I constantly check myself. I have taught students who have similar problems—it may be that one eye is stronger than the other or that (like me) they have an astigmatism. If you suffer from similar issues, do not worry because once you are aware of the problem you just need to remember to compensate for it when you are painting. And remember, there are many working artists who have made a virtue of the fact that they do not see in the same way as other people!

— Chapter 3 —

Recipes

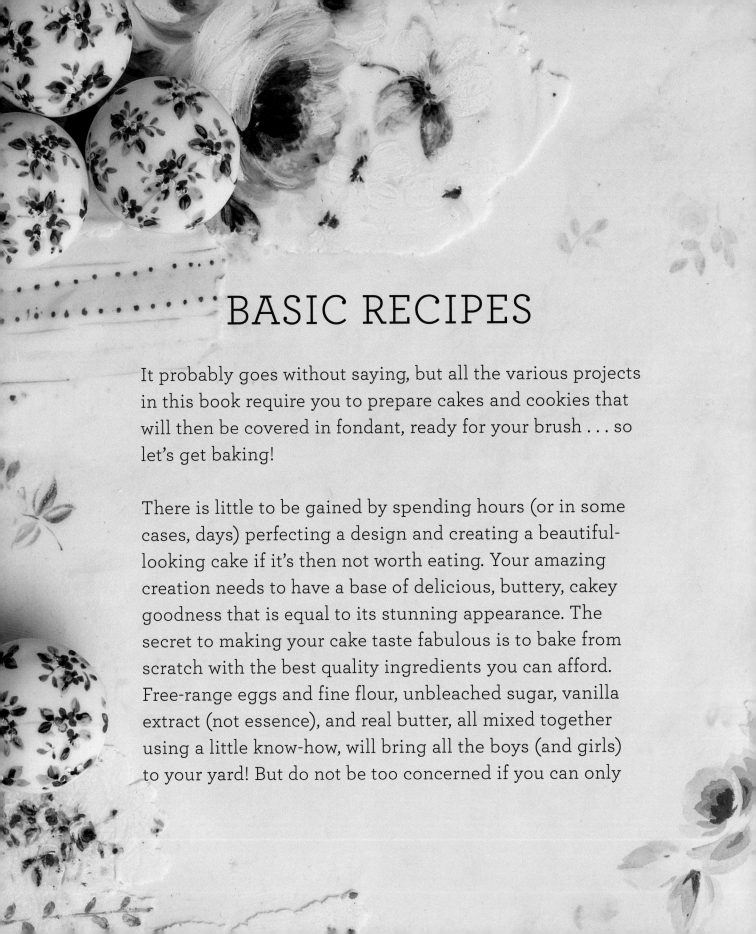

BASIC RECIPES

It probably goes without saying, but all the various projects in this book require you to prepare cakes and cookies that will then be covered in fondant, ready for your brush . . . so let's get baking!

There is little to be gained by spending hours (or in some cases, days) perfecting a design and creating a beautiful-looking cake if it's then not worth eating. Your amazing creation needs to have a base of delicious, buttery, cakey goodness that is equal to its stunning appearance. The secret to making your cake taste fabulous is to bake from scratch with the best quality ingredients you can afford. Free-range eggs and fine flour, unbleached sugar, vanilla extract (not essence), and real butter, all mixed together using a little know-how, will bring all the boys (and girls) to your yard! But do not be too concerned if you can only afford basic supplies—even making a cake from scratch using cheaper ingredients will always produce a superior result to a shop-bought cake (but always make sure to use butter rather than margarine).

Any firm cake should be suitable for covering in fondant. There's no particular recipe that you need to follow when making cakes you are planning to paint, but the recipes on the following pages are the ones I use most often, as they are simple to make and taste really delicious. If you have a favourite or foolproof cake recipe that always works for you, then, by all means, stick with it—just make sure that the final cake is dense enough to support the fondant.

For all the following recipes, you will need to use large eggs. Make sure that the eggs and butter are at room temperature because this will make it easier to combine the ingredients when making your cake.

CAKES

TRADITIONAL SPONGE CAKE

The recipe that follows is the one that I consistently use because it is so easy to whip up and tastes really delicious. It is made using equal amounts of sugar, butter, and flour (1¾ oz/50 g) for every egg used. I have provided the quantities of ingredients required to bake a cake *in a single tin* for a range of sizes. The cake is sliced into three layers, which are then filled with either buttercream or jam.

You may choose to bake your cakes in three separate (same-sized) tins—there are pros and cons for either method. With a single-tier cake, using three tins will drastically reduce the cooking time, and the cakes are less likely to be either burnt or undercooked. However, as each layer needs to be completely flat before it is covered, you now have three cakes to trim (rather than one), and you will be left with a lot more wasted cake.

Another issue arises with the three-tin method if you are creating a multiple-tiered cake, with separate tiers of different sizes (each tier split into three layers). With this method, you run into space problems in the oven—because you are using a separate tin for each layer, you can only bake a single tier of the cake at a time (as the oven will only take the three tins at once). But by using the one-tin method you can cook two tiers of cake at the same time, so the one-tin method may well be the quickest. (Don't bake more than two full tins at a time, though, as this can lead to uneven cooking.)

There are also two different methods for mixing the cake ingredients together. If you are making a small cake (6"/150 mm or less), or a single tray of cupcakes, the process will be much easier if you mix the batter using an electric hand-held whisk. But if you are beating up enough batter for larger cakes or big batches of cupcakes, you will need to bring out the big guns and invest in a table-top mixer.

As mentioned earlier, if your tins are even ¹⁄₃₂"/1 mm different in size to what is stated here this will affect the baking time. Just be aware of this and keep a careful eye on your cake when it is nearly finished baking.

Ingredient quantities and cooking times

4"/100 mm round cake: 3 eggs, 5½ oz/150 g each of unsalted butter, sugar, and self-raising flour, 1 teaspoon vanilla extract, milk. Cook for 40–50 minutes.

5"/130 mm round cake: 4 eggs, 7 oz/200 g each of unsalted butter, sugar, and self-raising flour, 1 teaspoon vanilla extract, milk. Cook for 50 minutes–1 hour.

6"/150 mm round cake: 5 eggs, 9 oz/250 g each of unsalted butter, sugar, and self-raising flour, 1 teaspoon vanilla extract, milk. Cook for 1–1¼ hours.

7"/180 mm round cake: 6 eggs, 10½ oz/300 g each of unsalted butter, sugar and self-raising flour, 1½ teaspoons vanilla extract, milk. Cook for 1¼–1¾ hours.

8"/200 mm round cake: 8 eggs, 14 oz/400g each of unsalted butter, sugar, and self-raising flour, 2 teaspoons vanilla extract, milk. Cook for 1 hour 45 minutes–1 hour 55 minutes.

9"/230 mm round cake: 10 eggs, 1 lb 2 oz/500 g each of unsalted butter, sugar, and self-raising flour, 2½ teaspoons vanilla extract, milk. Cook for 1 hour 50 minutes–2 hours 10 minutes.

10"/250 mm round cake: 12 eggs, 1 lb 5 oz/600 g each of unsalted butter, sugar, and self-raising flour, 3 teaspoons vanilla extract, milk. Cook for 2–2¼ hours..

4"/100 mm square cake: 3 eggs, 5¼ oz/150 g each of unsalted butter, sugar, and self-raising flour, 1 teaspoon vanilla extract, milk. Cook for 40–50 minutes.

6"/150 mm square cake: 6 eggs, 10½/300 g oz each of unsalted butter, sugar, and self-raising flour, 1½ teaspoons vanilla extract, milk. Cook for 1¼–1¾ hours.

8"/200 mm square cake: 12 eggs, 1 lb 5 oz/600 g each of unsalted butter, sugar, and self-raising flour, 3 teaspoons vanilla extract, milk. Cook for 2–2¼ hours.

Cupcakes
For a 12-cup tin: 3 eggs, 5½ oz/150 g each of unsalted butter, sugar, and self-raising flour, 1 teaspoon vanilla extract, milk. Cook for 15–20 minutes.

METHOD

Grease your cake tin and line it with parchment paper. Preheat the oven to 190°C/375°F/Gas 5/170°C fan. (If you have a fan selection on your oven, I would advise you to use this because it produces a more even bake. For other ovens, you may need to turn the cake to prevent one side cooking more quickly.)

HAND-WHISK METHOD

(not really suitable for cakes larger than 9"/230 mm)

1   Cream the butter and sugar together, for at least 5 minutes. The mixture should become noticeably paler and take on a fluffy appearance.

2   Add the eggs one at a time and beat them in well. If the mixture starts to curdle, add a dessertspoon of the flour and beat again.

3   Add the vanilla extract and mix in well.

4   Sieve the flour into the mixture.

5   Use a large spoon to gently fold in the flour.

6   Stir in enough milk to make a soft batter. It should be able to drop off a spoon fairly easily, but don't make it too runny.

TABLE-TOP MIXER METHOD

(not really suitable for cakes smaller than 6"/150 mm)

1   Place the butter and sugar in the mixing bowl. Break all the eggs into a separate bowl and add the vanilla extract, then weigh the flour into another bowl.

2   Cream the butter and sugar together until they become light and fluffy (as in the hand-whisk method above).

3   Add half the eggs to the butter and sugar mixture and beat until well mixed.

4   Add half the flour to the mixture, and beat again.

5   Add the rest of the eggs and beat as before.

6   Add the rest of the flour and beat until well mixed.

7   Add enough milk until the batter reaches the consistency required (see previous method). Use a spatula to scrape the bottom of the mixing bowl and get to any poorly mixed ingredients, then give the mixture one last beating.

For both methods

Spoon the batter into the prepared tin. (For cupcakes, divide the mixture between the 12 cases—the mixture should come to between half and two-thirds of the way up the side of the case.)

If you have a baking strip, put it around your tin.

Place the tin in the oven and bake for the required time. The cake is ready when a cake tester or skewer inserted into its centre comes out clean.

If you are baking cupcakes, brush them with warm sugar syrup as soon as they come out of the oven. This will help keep them moist (see page 64).

Leave the cake in the tin for 10 minutes and then turn it out onto a cooling tray. Make sure it is the right way up (sitting on its bottom rather than its top), or you may find it will crack and break up into bits.

Leave the cake to cool down completely, then take off the parchment paper, wrap the cake in plastic wrap or place it in an airtight tin. Leave overnight before filling and covering. Leaving the cake to rest ensures that it is less crumbly when you come to layer it.

FRUIT CAKE

It's probably because of all the Irish and Scottish DNA swimming about in my genes but I really, really love a traditional fruit cake. I always have an emergency fruit cake stashed away for when I'm craving some sugary goodness (which is all the time!)—the bonus is that with all the fruit squeezed into the cake it probably (definitely) counts as one of my five a day. Every now and then, I indulge in a good-sized chunk of the fruit cake with a sliver of mature cheddar cheese lying on top . . . it's surprisingly delicious.

This recipe is based on my nana's traditional fruit cake. I am very fortunate to have inherited her old recipe scrap book, and she had stuck at least twenty fruit cake recipes into the now-faded pages. But this particular one is her family recipe, which has been used for many generations. My mother made my wedding cake using this recipe, in the same way that her mother had made her cake. I have tweaked it a little though, because my nana was a strict teetotaller and so she would have soaked the fruit in orange juice rather than brandy, I'm not sure that she would have approved of my extensive alcohol selection (all for baking purposes, of course!).

One of the lovely features of a fruit cake is that you can really play around with the ingredients. You don't need to stick to the same dried fruit that I have used. Feel free to let your imagination run wild—just make sure that you're using the same total weight of fruit as the original recipe. You could substitute dried blueberries or cranberries to create a New World flavour. Or add dates, figs or crystallised ginger if you want a more spicy and exotic flavour. My recipe does not include any nuts (apart from the marzipan), but walnuts, pecans, or almonds would all be suitable ingredients to add to the dried fruit. You can also change the type of alcohol you use to soak the fruit. You need one that has a good strong flavour, so avoid vodka, but whisky, rum, sherry, or even a fruit liqueur would work really well.

Fruit cakes need to be cooked at a low temperature to prevent the fruit from scorching and burning. Therefore, they will take a long time to cook—up to five hours depending on their size. So be sure to make your fruit cake when you know you will be near your oven for a while. Often I put my cake in the oven only to realise that I have an appointment three hours later, just when I should be taking the cake out.

This type of cake is best made at least one month (but preferably three months) before it is eaten. This is so that the cake will mature in flavour—and you can "feed" the cake with your chosen alcohol to make an even richer, moister cake. To feed the cake, prick the top all over with a cocktail stick and then pour on two teaspoons of your chosen alcohol. Do this every week, then wrap the cake back up and put it back into a tin.

I have described two methods for making the cake, either by using a hand whisk or with a table-top mixer. Even large fruit cakes are much easier to mix by hand compared with a sponge cake, because the fruit is held together with a relatively small amount of batter, so it is easier to mix larger cakes with an electric hand whisk. With very large cakes I then transfer the batter to an even larger bowl which will accommodate all the fruit.

Ingredient quantities and cooking times

4"/100 mm round cake: 1 egg, 2¾ oz/75 g each of unsalted butter, dark brown sugar, and plain (all-purpose) flour, ½ teaspoon each of ground ginger, ground cinnamon and mixed spice, ¼ teaspoon grated nutmeg, pinch of salt, grated zest of ½ orange and ½ lemon, 5½ oz/150 g currants, 2¾ oz/75 g each of sultanas (golden raisins) and raisins, 1 oz/25 g each of mixed peel and glacé cherries, ½ fl oz/ 20 ml brandy (or other alcohol). Cook for 2—2¼ hours.

5"/125 mm round cake: 2 eggs, 3½ oz/100 g each of unsalted butter, dark brown sugar, and plain (all-purpose) flour, ½ teaspoon each of ground ginger, ground cinnamon, and mixed spice, ¼ teaspoon grated nutmeg, pinch of salt, grated zest of ½ orange and ½ lemon, 9 oz/250 g currants, 3½ oz/100 g each of sultanas (golden raisins) and raisins, 1¾ oz/50 g each of mixed peel and glacé cherries, ½ fl oz/20 ml brandy (or other alcohol). Cook for 2½—3 hours.

6"/150 mm round cake: 3 eggs, 5½ oz/150 g each of unsalted butter, dark brown sugar, and plain (all-purpose) flour, 1 teaspoon each of ground ginger, ground cinnamon, and mixed spice, ¼ teaspoon grated nutmeg, pinch of salt, grated zest of 1 orange and 1 lemon, 10½ oz/300 g currants, 5½ oz/150 g sultanas (golden raisins), 3½ oz/100 g raisins, 2¾ oz/75 g each of mixed peel and glacé cherries, 1 fl oz/30 ml brandy (or other alcohol). Cook for 3—3½ hours.

7"/180 mm round cake: 3 eggs, 6 oz/175 g each of unsalted butter, dark brown sugar, and plain (all-purpose) flour, 1 teaspoon each of ground ginger, ground cinnamon, and mixed spice, ½ teaspoon grated nutmeg, pinch of salt, grated zest of 1 orange and 1 lemon, 13 oz/375 g currants, 6 oz/175 g sultanas (golden raisins), 3½ oz/100 g each of raisins, mixed peel and glacé cherries, 1¼ fl oz/40 ml brandy (or other alcohol). Cook for 3½—4 hours.

8"/200 mm round cake: 4 eggs, 8 oz/225 g each of unsalted butter, dark brown sugar, and plain (all-purpose) flour, 1 teaspoon each of ground ginger, ground cinnamon, and mixed spice, ½ teaspoon grated nutmeg, pinch of salt, grated zest of 1 orange and 1 lemon, 1 lb 2 oz/500 g currants, 8 oz/225 g sultanas (golden raisins), 4½ oz/125 g each of raisins, mixed peel and glacé cherries, 1¼ fl oz/40 ml brandy (or other alcohol). Cook for 4—4½ hours.

9"/230 mm round cake: 6 eggs, 11½ oz/325 g each of unsalted butter, dark brown sugar, and plain (all-purpose) flour, 1½ teaspoons each of ground ginger, ground cinnamon, and mixed spice, 1 teaspoon grated nutmeg, pinch of salt, grated zest of 2 oranges and 1 lemon, 1 lb 10 oz/750 g currants, 11½ oz/325 g sultanas (golden raisins), 6 oz/175 g each of raisins, mixed peel and glacé cherries, 2 fl oz/60 ml brandy (or other alcohol). Cook for 4½—5 hours.

10"/250 mm round cake: 8 eggs, 1 lb/450 g each of unsalted butter, dark brown sugar, and plain (all-purpose) flour, 2 teaspoons each of ground ginger, ground cinnamon, and mixed spice, ½ teaspoon grated nutmeg, large pinch of salt, grated zest of 2 oranges and 2 lemons, 2 lb 4 oz/1 kg currants, 1 lb/450 g sultanas (golden raisins), 9 oz/250 g each of raisins, mixed peel and glacé cherries, 2½ fl oz/80 ml brandy (or other alcohol). Cook for 5—5½ hours.

4"/100 mm square cake: 2 eggs, 3½ oz/100 g each of unsalted butter, dark brown sugar, and plain (all-purpose) flour, ½ teaspoon each of ground ginger, ground cinnamon, and mixed spice, ¼ teaspoon grated nutmeg, pinch of salt, grated zest of ½ orange and ½ lemon, 9 oz/250 g currants, 3½ oz/100 g sultanas (golden raisins), 2¾ oz/75 g raisins, 1¾ oz/50 g each of mixed peel and glacé cherries, ½ fl oz/20 ml brandy (or other alcohol). Cook for 2½—3 hours.

6"/150 mm square cake: 3 eggs, 6 oz/175 g each of unsalted butter, dark brown sugar, and plain (all-purpose) flour, 1 teaspoon each of ground ginger, ground cinnamon, and mixed spice, ½ teaspoon grated nutmeg, pinch of salt, grated zest of 1 orange and 1 lemon, 13 oz/375 g currants, 6 oz/175 g sultanas (golden raisins), 3½ oz/100 g each of raisins, mixed peel and glacé cherries, 1¼ fl oz/40 ml brandy (or other alcohol). Cook for 3¼—3½ hours.

8"/200 mm square cake: 6 eggs, 11½ oz/325 g each of unsalted butter, dark brown sugar and plain (all-purpose) flour, 1½ teaspoons each of ground ginger, ground cinnamon and mixed spice, 1 teaspoon grated nutmeg, pinch of salt, grated zest of 2 oranges and 1 lemon, 1 lb 10 oz/750 g currants, 11½ oz/325 g sultanas (golden raisins), 6 oz/175 g each of raisins, mixed peel and glacé cherries, 2 fl oz/60 ml brandy (or other alcohol). Cook for 4—4½ hours.

Cupcakes

For a 12-cup tin: 3 eggs, 5½ oz/150 g each of unsalted butter, dark brown sugar, and plain (all-purpose) flour, 1 teaspoon each of ground ginger, ground cinnamon, and mixed spice, ¼ teaspoon grated nutmeg, pinch of salt, grated zest of 1 orange and 1 lemon, 10½ oz/300 g currants, 5½ oz/150 g sultanas (golden raisins), 3½ oz/100 g raisins, 2¾ oz/75 g each of mixed peel and glacé cherries, 1 fl oz/30 ml brandy (or other alcohol. Cook for 45 minutes—1 hour.

METHOD

Twenty-four hours before you wish to bake your cake, put all the dried fruit in a large bowl. Pour over enough boiling water to cover the fruit completely—this will really plump it up and help it absorb the alcohol. Leave for ten minutes, then drain off all the water. Then add the brandy (or fruit juice if you do not want to use alcohol) to the now plumped fruit. Mix in well, cover the bowl and leave at least overnight, or until you start baking.

- The first step for both methods is to preheat the oven to 150°C/350°F/Gas 2/130°C fan. Prepare the cake tin: grease the tin with butter, then line it with double thickness parchment paper.

HAND-WHISK METHOD

1   Sift the flour, spices, and salt together into a bowl.

2   Cream the butter and sugar together until the mixture is lighter in colour and takes on a more fluffy appearance.

3   Add the eggs one at a time, beating the mixture after each addition. If your cake batter starts to separate and curdle, add a small amount of the flour mixture with each egg. Do not be too concerned if this happens—the cake will still be amazing.

4   Using a large spoon, fold in the flour.

5   Add the orange and lemon zest and mix in well. Add the fruit. Gently fold into the mixture until well mixed.

TABLE-TOP MIXER METHOD

1   Sift the flour, spices, and salt together.

2   Place the butter and sugar in the mixing bowl. Break all the eggs into a separate bowl.

3   Cream the butter and sugar together until it is light and fluffy (see previous method).

4   Add half of the eggs and beat until well mixed.

5   Add half the flour, and again beat well.

6   Add the rest of the eggs and beat as before.

7   Add the rest of the flour and beat until well mixed.

8   Add the orange and lemon zest and beat them into the mixture.

9   Remove the bowl from the stand and add the fruit. Stir the fruit into the mixture using a large spoon until well combined.

For both methods

Transfer the mixture to the tin and cover the top with a circle of parchment paper (make it slightly larger than the circumference of the tin—this is to protect the top of the cake and prevent the fruit from scorching).

If you are making cupcakes, divide the mixture between the 12 cases. They will be very full, but don't be concerned as fruit cakes don't rise in the same way a sponge cake does. Cupcakes don't need to be covered with parchment paper because the bake time is quite short.

Bake for the specified time. When the cake is ready, its surface will be a rich golden brown and a skewer inserted into the cake will come out cleanly.

When you take the cake out of the oven, prick its surface using a cocktail stick. Then baste the cake with 1 tablespoon of brandy.

Leave the cake to cool in its tin for 20 minutes and then turn out onto a cooling tray.

Once the cake has cooled, wrap it in greaseproof paper and then either tin foil or plastic wrap. Then place it in a cake tin.

Every week or two unwrap the cake and baste it with brandy, then re-cover and leave the cake to mature.

COOKIES

If you were to sneak into my house whenever my children's birthday parties are in full swing and peek into one of the party bags, you would always find a cookie hidden away among the cake and plastic tat. Normally it is painted to match the theme chosen for that particular party—it could be a cowgirl, a monkey, or even a cookie of an underwater scene.

A painted cookie can make a really attractive wedding favour, and if you were to paint a name on it, then it could double as an edible name tag for a table place setting. Even the simplest cookie packaged in a cellophane wrapper, tied with a beautiful ribbon and maybe even presented with a matching tag, will look fabulous enough to grace any event.

I try hard not to keep my cookie repertoire limited to pretty flowers—much as I do love painting them. During my decorating career, I have painted many different types of images onto cookies, including some that are quite bizarre, ranging from portraits of celebrities, fish heads and bones, TV remote controls, to the influenza virus and severed toes.

There is something of a balancing act to be made when baking cookies. Obviously, the end product needs to be fabulously tasty, but you also require a cookie that doesn't spread too much while it's cooking. This is done by adjusting the ratio of butter and flour. The more butter in a cookie mix, then the crisper and tastier the final product, but too much butter will cause the cookie to spread and lose its shape. Adding flour will help stabilise the cookie, but too much will create a product that is tough and inedible.

If you find that your cookies are spreading too much, there are a few things that you can do about this

- Make sure that the butter you are using in the recipe is not too soft. You do need it to be softened (at room temperature), but if it is melted when you mix it in, your cookie will spread. (This is not relevant for the gingerbread recipe because the butter is melted as part of the mix.)

- Use a butter with a lower water content—sadly, these generally will be the more expensive brands.

- Do not overbeat the butter and sugar: do not "cream" them together as you would when making a cake—but as soon as they have combined, stop beating. (Not relevant for gingerbread cookies.)

- Make sure that you are properly resting your dough, first after mixing and then after cutting out. You can leave the dough in the fridge overnight to rest, or even place it in the freezer until you need it.

- If you increase the temperature of the oven, the cookies will cook in a quicker time and therefore are less likely to spread. However, you run the risk of burning the outside while the centre is undercooked, so keep a careful eye on the cookies while they are baking.

- As a last resort, if you have tried all the above and your dough is still spreading too much during cooking, then add more flour to your mixture.

If you are using a hand whisk, beat the butter and sugar together and then mix in the egg. But because the following recipes create such a stiff dough, I suggest you mix in the flour with a wooden spoon.

BASIC VANILLA COOKIES

This recipe errs on the side of taste, so you will find it spreads a little. This should not be a problem because the cookie will keep its shape enough to be able to decorate it. This is best made using a table-top mixer.

8 oz/225 g unsalted butter
7 oz/200 g caster (superfine) sugar
1 egg
1 teaspoon vanilla extract
13 oz/375 g plain (all-purpose) flour

METHOD

1   Beat together the butter and sugar, until just combined.

2   Add the egg and vanilla extract and beat the mixture again.

3   While the beater is running on a low setting, gradually add the flour.

4   Stop mixing as soon as the dough has come together.

5   Take the dough out of the bowl and pat it into a flattened cake shape.

6   Wrap the dough in plastic wrap and place in the fridge for at least an hour, but preferably overnight.

7   Preheat your oven to 190°C/375°F/Gas 5/170°C fan. (If you are not using the fan setting, you will need to turn the baking tray halfway through the baking time to achieve an even bake.) Line your baking trays with parchment paper.

8   Roll the dough out using spacers to set the thickness, then cut out the dough with your chosen cutters or use a scalpel to cut around a template.

9   Place the cookies on prepared baking trays, then leave them in the fridge for 30 minutes–1 hour.

10   Place the baking trays in the preheated oven and bake for 12–15 minutes (baking times depend on the size of your cookies—the larger the cookies, the longer they will take to cook, and very small cookies will take less time), until the cookies are slightly brown on the edges and firm in the middle. Leave the cookies to cool for about 10 minutes, then transfer them to a cooling tray.

11   There's no need to cover the cookies in fondant straight away; you can store them in an airtight tin for up to a week before you need to cover them in fondant when you are ready to decorate them.

For chocolate cookies, substitute 1¾ oz/ 50 g of cocoa powder for the same weight of flour.

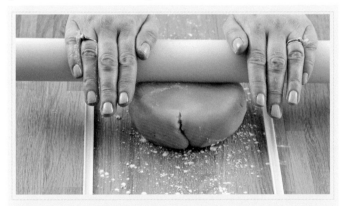

How to use spacers
1 Lightly flour (using flour for cookie dough, cornflour (cornstarch) for marzipan or fondant) the work surface.
2 Place the spacers parallel to each other with the dough/marzipan/fondant in between. Make sure the distance between the spacers is less than the length of your rolling pin.
3 Roll out the dough/marzipan/fondant until you cannot roll any further. It will have reached the height of the spacers and should be an even thickness.

GINGERBREAD COOKIES

The distinctive smell of gingerbread wafting through the house is guaranteed to transport me back to my childhood. I can vividly remember making giant cookies with my dad while my mum was away visiting her family in Ireland. I made a wonky giraffe and decorated it with runny icing and sweets, while my brother fashioned an elephant with chocolate buttons and liquorice allsorts. I can't recall eating it to tell you how it tasted, but I can still picture it in my mind's eye.

The recipe I have created for you to use with these painting projects has a lovely complex spicy flavour, but if you're worried it may be a little too sophisticated for younger taste buds, then reduce the cinnamon and ginger quantities to 1 teaspoon of each, and substitute mixed spice for the allspice.

This is best made using a table-top mixer. If you don't have one then for the sake of your hand whisk, I suggest you stir the flour into the sugar/syrup mixture with a wooden spoon until well combined.

7 oz/200 g unsalted butter

7 oz/ 200 g dark muscovado sugar

2 tablespoons syrup

2 tablespoons honey

1 tablespoon ground cinnamon

1 tablespoon ground ginger

1 teaspoon allspice

½ teaspoon salt

1 teaspoon bicarbonate of soda (baking soda)

1 tablespoon water

14 oz/400 g plain (all-purpose) flour

METHOD

1 Put the butter, sugar, syrup, honey, spices and salt in a saucepan and gently heat together over low heat until the butter has melted and the sugar has dissolved, then take the pan off the heat.

2 In a small bowl, dissolve the bicarbonate of soda in the water. Add this to the ingredients in the pan and stir well until combined. Pour the resulting mixture into the bowl of the mixer.

3 Add the flour. Use a low setting on the mixer to combine the liquid and flour until it has formed a stiff dough.

4 Stop mixing as soon as the dough has come together.

5 Take the dough out of the bowl and pat it into a flattened cake shape.

6 Wrap the dough in plastic wrap and place it in the refrigerator for at least an hour, but preferably overnight.

7 Preheat your oven to 190°C/375°F/Gas 5/170°C fan. (If you are not using the fan setting, you will need to turn the baking tray halfway through the baking time to achieve an even bake.) Line your baking trays with parchment paper.

8 Roll the dough out using spacers to set the thickness, then cut out the shapes with your chosen cutters or use a scalpel to cut around a template.

9 Place the cookies on prepared baking trays, then leave them in the refrigerator for 30 minutes–1 hour before baking.

10 Place the baking trays in the preheated oven, and, again depending on the size of your cookies, bake for 12–15 minutes, until the cookies are slightly brown on the edges and firm in the middle.

11 Leave the cookies to cool for about 10 minutes, then transfer them to a cooling tray.

12 You can store the cookies in an airtight tin for up to a week before you need to cover them in fondant when you are ready to decorate them.

HOW TO MAKE COOKIE POPS

To transform a humble cookie into something much more exciting (a cookie pop) is really, really easy. Just be sure to source cookie sticks that are suitable for baking (some sticks are plastic and will melt in the oven). Happily, most sugarcraft shops or online suppliers will stock the ones you need.

You can get different lengths of sticks: for most cookies I use a 6"/150 mm stick unless the stick itself is part of the overall design (for example, if I'm making a fairy or wizard wand), in which case I would use an 8"/200 mm or 10"/250 mm stick. Generally speaking, a stick smaller than 6"/150 mm is impractical and can also look a little odd.

Roll out your cookie dough in the same manner as described in the Vanilla Cookie recipe (page 60), and cut out your chosen shape. Place one finger on top of the cookie, over the area where you are going to insert the stick (normally the midpoint at the base of the shape), then gently push the cookie stick into the side of the cookie, making sure it is going cleanly into the shape and that there is enough cookie dough above and below the stick to support it (in other words, make sure it hasn't gone into the dough at an angle). Usually I'll insert the stick until it is between half and two-thirds of the way up the cookie. Then turn the cookie over so that you can check the back; if you can see the stick coming through the surface, then take a small amount of dough and cover the exposed area. Place the cookies on a baking tray lined with parchment paper, making sure that the sticks are lying flat, and bake as usual.

After baking, be sure to transfer the cookies to a cooling tray very carefully—use a spatula to lift the cookie. If you try to pick them up using the stick (before they have cooled), you may find the cookie cracking and breaking. Once they have cooled they will harden and you can pick them up by the stick without any fear of breakages.

Cookie dough

Carefully insert the stick into the dough

FILLINGS, PASTES AND FONDANTS

SUGAR SYRUP

Before you layer and fill a sponge cake with buttercream, it's a good idea to brush each layer with a sugar syrup. This will keep your cake moist.

The recipe for sugar syrup is very simple: just add a measurement of sugar (in ounces/grams) to an equal amount of water (in fl oz/ml)—so, for example, you would mix 1¾ oz/50 g of sugar with 1¾ fl oz/50 ml water. You place the ingredients in a saucepan and gently heat. When the sugar has dissolved into the water, the syrup is ready. Don't stir the mixture as it heats or it will form crystals.

Similarly, when you cover a fruit cake with marzipan and fondant, you'll find that a sugar syrup can help to form a sticky surface for the marzipan to adhere to. You can use a simple sugar-and-water mix here, using the recipe above—but for extra richness and flavour, you could replace the water with alcohol (the same type you used in the cake). Of course, if you prefer the traditional method, then you can always use an apricot preserve.

If you are making sponge cupcakes, you can brush them with warm syrup as soon as they come out of the oven. The syrup will soak into the sponge, keeping it moist for longer.

Quantities of sugar syrup for different-sized cakes
Round cakes

4"/100 mm – ½ fl oz/20 ml, 5"/130 mm – 1 fl oz/30 ml, 6"/150 mm – 1¾ fl oz/ 50 ml, 7"/180 mm – 2 fl oz/60 ml, 8"/200 mm – 3 fl oz/90 ml, 9"/230 mm – 4½ fl oz/130 ml, 10"/250 mm – 5 fl oz/150 ml

Square cakes

4"/100 mm – ½ fl oz/20 ml, 6"/150 mm – 2 fl oz/60 ml, 8"/200 mm – 3½ fl oz/100 ml, 10"/250 mm – 5½ fl oz/170 ml

12 cupcakes

1 fl oz/30 ml

JAM/PRESERVE

For most sponge cakes (other than chocolate), I fill one layer with jam or preserve. This can add a lovely tang to the cake and prevent it from being overly sweet. Traditionally, vanilla sponges are filled with strawberry or raspberry jam, but if I'm making a lemon cake I will use lemon curd, or I will use marmalade for an orange-flavoured cake.

Every now and then (if I am being especially virtuous), I will make my own jam, but most of the time I use a ready-made product. You can easily find a good-quality jam on the shelves of your nearest supermarket, or scout out a more unusual flavoured preserve at your local farmers market.

Quantities of jam for different-sized cakes
Round cakes

4"/100 mm – 2 teaspoons, 5"/130 mm – 3 teaspoons, 6"/150 mm – 3 dessertspoons , 7"/180 mm – 4 dessertspoons, 8"/200 mm – 5 dessertspoons (roughly half a jar), 9"/230 mm – 7 dessertspoons, 10"/250 mm – 8 dessertspoons

Square cakes

4"/100 mm – 3 teaspoons, 6"/150 mm – 4 dessertspoons, 8"/200 mm – 7 dessertspoons, 10"/250 mm – 11 dessertspoons (a whole 13 oz/370 g jar)

BUTTERCREAM

To make the buttercream, you'll need to beat together equal amounts of butter and icing (confectioners') sugar (the butter should be at room temperature)—for example, if the recipe calls for 3½ oz/100 g buttercream, then you'll need to mix 1¾ oz/50 g butter with 1¾ oz/50 g icing sugar.

Cream the butter and icing sugar together until the mixture is really light and fluffy. If you want to make a flavoured icing, add 1 teaspoon of flavouring (such as vanilla extract or lemon juice) for every 3½ oz/100 g of buttercream. If you want to make a chocolate buttercream, then substitute a quarter of the weight of icing sugar for cocoa powder.

Quantities of buttercream for different-sized cakes
Round cakes
4"/100 mm – 7 oz/200 g, 5"/130 mm – 9 oz/250 g,
6"/150 mm – 12 oz/350 g, 7"/180 mm – 1 lb 2 oz/500 g,
8"/200 mm – 1 lb 7 oz/650 g, 9"/230 mm – 1 lb 14 oz/
850 g, 10"/250 mm – 2 lb 4oz/1 kg

Square Cakes
4"/100 mm – 7 oz/200 g, 6"/150 mm – 1 lb 4 oz/550 g,
8"/200 mm – 1 kg

12 cupcakes
covered with buttercream swirls – 1 lb 2 oz/500 g
covered with fondant – 14 oz/400 g

MARZIPAN

I always cover a fruit cake with commercially made
marzipan. Of course, you can make your own, but there
are only so many hours in my day. I much prefer the
natural-coloured marzipan, but the yellow variety is
perfectly acceptable.

Leftover marzipan can be collected together, wrapped
in plastic wrap and stored in the freezer until needed.

Quantities of marzipan for different-sized cakes
Round cakes
4"/100 mm – 12 oz/350 g, 5"/130 mm – 1 lb 2 oz/500 g,
6"/150 mm – 1 lb 5 oz/600 g, 7"/180 mm – 1 lb 12 oz/800 g,
8"/200 mm – 2 lb 4 oz/1 kg, 9"/230 mm – 2 lb 12 oz/
1.25 kg, 10"/250 mm – 3 lb 2½ oz/1.45 kg

Square cakes
4"/100 mm – 1 lb 2 oz/500 g, 6"/150 mm – 1 lb 10 oz/
750 g, 8"/200 mm – 2 lb 4 oz/1 kg

12 cupcakes
1 lb/450 g

SUGAR PASTE/FONDANT

For all of the projects you will work through in this book,
when the instructions call for you to use fondant, then

I am referring to the sugar paste that you roll out and
use to cover a cake (not the liquid icing that you dip
cupcakes into, or pour over French fancies). I always use
commercial, ready-made, ready to roll fondant: I have tried
fondant from many different producers and they have all
been suitable for painting on. I've never used homemade
fondant, so I can't comment on its properties—but if you
normally make your own, then I suggest you experiment
on a tester piece first, just to make sure the surface will
happily take paint without any issues.

Most supermarkets now stock fondant, normally in
packets of 2 lb 4 oz/1 kg. You can buy larger quantities
from specialist cake-decorating suppliers or from the
manufacturer. Try a few different brands until you find
one that you like working with.

In the quantities below, I have specified more fondant
than is needed to cover the cake. This is because, as well
as covering the cake, you need some spare fondant at the
bottom, to ensure the covering fits well. This small skirt
of material around the base of the cake is deliberately
there so that you can carefully lift and repair any folds to
create a perfect smooth covering—this process is covered
later. This is just to warn you not to be surprised if you
find you have plenty of spare fondant after covering your
cake.

Quantities of fondant for different-sized cakes
Round cakes
4"/100 mm – 14 oz/400 g, 5"/130 mm – 1 lb/450 g,
6"/150 mm – 1 lb 5 oz/600 g, 7"/180 mm – 1 lb 9 oz/700 g,
8"/200 mm – 1 lb 12 oz/800 g, 9"/230 mm – 2 lb 2 oz/950 g,
10"/250 mm – 2 lb 12 oz/1.25 kg

Square cakes
4"/100 mm – 14 oz/400 g, 6"/150 mm – 1 lb 10 oz/750 g,
8"/200 mm – 2 lb/900 g

Double barrel
5"/130 mm cake – 2 lb/900 g

12 cupcakes
1 lb 4 oz/550 g

METHOD FOR MAKING COLOURED FONDANT

Using a cocktail stick to pick up a little of your chosen colour, add a small amount at a time to the fondant and knead it well with your hands. Keep adding more colour until you have the achieved the tone you need.

If you are making a strong colour, this can sometimes affect the consistency of the fondant. Once you have mixed up the colour, leave the fondant, covered in plastic wrap, for a few hours before you use it.

MODELLING PASTE

To create painted cut-outs or cupcake toppers, you will need to use a fondant that is stronger and dries harder than the normal sugar paste. I mix my own modelling paste by using Gum Tragacanth ("gum trag"), but you can also use CMC, which is sometimes known as Tylose or Tylo powder. You can purchase either of these products from a specialist cake-decorating supplier (or you can buy ready-made modelling paste).

METHOD FOR MAKING MODELLING PASTE

Knead 1 teaspoon of either gum trag or CMC into 9 oz/250 g of fondant with your hands. If you are using gum trag you will need to leave the modelling paste overnight, wrapped in plastic wrap. Modelling paste made using CMC can be used immediately—there's no need to let it rest.

As a rule I prefer using gum trag, which is a purely personal choice—I have always found it easier to work with. However, CMC is incredibly handy for the times when you forget to mix up your modelling paste the day before you need to use it.

Colour modelling paste using the same method as described above for fondant. However, because the gum trag or CMC stabilises the paste, you can use it immediately after colouring.

PETAL PASTE

If you want to create a thinner cut-out or plaque than one you can make with the standard modelling paste, then use petal paste—I have only ever used the ready-made variety (specialist cake-decorating suppliers will stock this). However, you need to cut out the shape of your flower (or other element) first, and then let the paste dry completely before you begin to paint. If you paint onto the petal paste before it has dried, you will find that the surface of the paste becomes slimy, and that it is hard to create any beautiful marks.

CONFECTIONERS' GLUE

You can buy ready-made confectioners' glue from cake-decorating suppliers, but it's really easy to make your own: just sprinkle ¼ teaspoon of gum trag or CMC powder over 1¾ fl oz/50 ml water. Leave it for 10 minutes, until it has soaked up some of the water and turned into a gel, and then stir it all together with a paintbrush. I normally use CMC for this as the resulting glue is clearer; the glue created with gum trag has a more opaque quality and a slight brownish tone. You can keep your confectioners' glue in the fridge for a week after mixing—if you find that it becomes too thick to use then just stir in a little more water.

ROYAL ICING

I always use fondant to cover cookies or to create plaques, but you can, if you prefer, use royal icing instead. Just be sure that it is completely dry before you start any painting. Using royal icing will result in a slightly different finish on the final product from the result you get using fondant, so experiment first to make certain you will end up with the results you want.

You can also use royal icing for sticking elements to a cake if you wish, rather than the confectioners' glue.

If I ever need to use royal icing, I use a ready-mix packet so all that I need to add is the water. Most supermarkets will stock this.

However if you wish to make your own, then you can use this recipe.

1 oz/25 g powdered egg white (you can find this in the baking aisle of most supermarkets)

2 lb 4 oz/1 kg icing (confectioners') sugar

5¼ fl oz/160 ml of water

METHOD FOR MAKING ROYAL ICING

1 Put the powdered egg white and icing sugar in a bowl and mix well together.

2 Gradually add the water and beat until the icing has reached the required consistency (this can take up to 10 minutes).

3 Store the icing in an airtight container until required. It will keep for up to a week if refrigerated, but you will need to beat it again before you use it.

Chapter 4

Preparing your Canvas

PREPARING CAKES AND COOKIES FOR PAINTING

In the same manner that artists prepare their canvas for painting, you will need to take some time to make sure that your fondant is ready before you can begin painting. Cakes need to be layered and filled before they are covered, and then given structural support if they are to be tiered. Cupcakes must be covered in fondant, or given a buttercream swirl so that a pre-made topper can be used as the decoration that you'll paint on. Cookies are the simplest of these confections to prepare, as they are ready for painting after only a covering of fondant.

The methods described in this chapter are those that I have developed over the years, on many cake-making projects, to achieve the perfect finish on the fondant ready for painting. In that time, I have picked up many tips from fellow cake decorators, from books, and from trawling the internet, and some I have just discovered myself through a lot of trial and error. But I have never received any formal sugarcraft training, so if you think that you already have a foolproof way to achieve a flawless finish, then by all means, stick with it! Nonetheless, I would encourage you to read my instructions on covering cakes with fondant because there are some normal practices that people customarily follow that are not suitable for use with painting techniques.

PREPARING THE CAKE BOARD

At least one day before I cover the cake, I prepare the cake board. This is to give the fondant on it sufficient time to firm up, making it less likely to mark or dent when you put the cake on top. I usually use a board that is 2"/50 mm bigger than the cake I am using (this ratio seems visually appealing) so an 8"/200 mm cake would be presented on a 10"/250 mm cake board. If making a tiered cake, then I use the size of the bottom tier to calculate the size of board required. Sometimes, if I'm working on a smaller cake (such as a 6"/150 mm one), I can get away with using a cake board that is just 1"/25 mm bigger, but for anything larger, a 2"/50 mm difference in size will be perfect. Using a board that is wider than the cake also helps protect any decoration on the side of the cake if you are transporting it in a box.

Now, I don't want to give you the false impression that I'm always organised enough to prepare my cake boards ahead of time. But fortunately I have a fall-back plan in place for the times when I remember too late in the day that I need a covered board: Remember the CMC I mentioned in the ingredients list? Well, if time is short, then before you roll out your fondant make sure to knead some CMC powder into it. Once the board is covered, the fondant will firm up within an hour.

Roll out the fondant using your spacers, so that it is slightly bigger than the board you want to use. Lightly moisten the cake board with water. Place the fondant on top of the board and smooth it over with the smoothers. Trim the edges so that the fondant is flush with the edge of the board.

Then you need to cover the edge of the board so that it is hidden. The usual way to do this is with a ribbon. Stick a strip of double-sided tape around the edge of the board and then stick the ribbon onto that. If you are using a particularly thick ribbon or one made from natural or rougher fibres, you may need to use a glue gun to attach it to the board. Of course, you don't need to use a ribbon—there are plenty of other options. You could cut a strip of patterned paper or fabric to cover the edge (why not make a feature of the frayed edge of the fabric?) or anything, really: I have been using washi tape more and more recently as it comes in such fabulous patterns and is really easy to use.

Cutting with a cake leveller

Trimming with a cake leveller

Creating a buttercream ledge

LAYERING A CAKE

After baking, leave the cake overnight before you layer and fill it because it needs this time to settle. If you try to fill it before it has settled, then you may find it too crumbly to work with.

When I fill a sponge cake, I normally use a jam or preserve for one of the layers of filling, and buttercream for the other. This is just a personal preference—I find the jam adds a tartness to the cake, which is a lovely contrast to the soft sweetness of the buttercream. You can, if you prefer, use two layers of buttercream (I do this when I'm layering a chocolate sponge), but if so, bear in mind that you will need to increase the buttercream quantities given in the previous chapter for the different cake sizes.

To cut the layers, I find it easiest to use a cake leveller—it keeps each layer totally flat, and so any tiered cake will be more stable and less likely to fall over. For a cake with two fillings, cut the cake into three layers: you set the depth of slice you want and keep it at the same depth for all three layers so that they are equal. This creates a great-looking cake, even after it has been cut for serving.

If you are using a serrated knife to cut your layers, then use a measure to keep track of the depth you need for each layer (normally about ¾"/20 mm) as you carefully cut around the cake—this will help ensure that each layer is even and level all the way across. You can measure the depth of cake you require and stick a cocktail stick into the cake at this point. Repeat this process around the cake, so that you have visual markers showing where you should cut the cake. Remove the sticks once you have created the layer.

Before you fill the cake, brush each layer with the sugar syrup as this will help to keep the cake moist.

METHOD

1   Take the layer that was the top of the cake, turn it over and place it on a cake board (one that is at least 2"/50 mm wider than the cake) so that the part of the cake that was at the top will be the base of the finished cake (this means that the roughest surface— the one that you have cut—will be hidden at the base of the cake). Place the cake (still on the board) onto a turntable.

2   Using a spatula or palette knife, create a ledge of buttercream around the edge of this first layer. This will hold the jam in place and stop it from mixing with the frosting on the outside. Then spread the jam over the cake up to the buttercream.

Preparing the second layer

Covering top and side with buttercream

Smoothing crumb coat with a cake scraper

3 Take the middle cake layer and place it carefully on top of the bottom layer.

4 Make a second ledge of buttercream on the top of this new layer, then add a good dollop of buttercream in the middle and spread it to the edge.

5 Next take the final remaining layer, turn it upside down and place it on top of the rest of the cake (this gives you a good flat top and a nice sharp edge to work with).

6 Spread a layer of buttercream over the top and side of the cake with your knife—this is called a "crumb coat" because it seals in any crumbs on the surface of the cake. Then take a cake scraper and run it around the side of the cake to create a flat surface of buttercream. The side of the cake needs to be straight and at a 90° angle to the board (this is to give you the best possible surface on which to place your fondant). Then use a palette knife to smooth out the top surface of the cake. Again, this needs to be as flat as possible—make sure the edge of the cake has a good clean line.

7 Place the cake in the fridge for half an hour, until the buttercream has hardened.

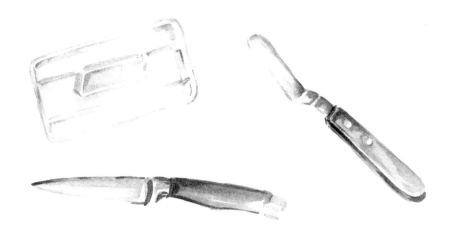

Lightly sprinkle the surface with cornflour

Roll out the fondant

Smooth the surface

COVERING A CAKE WITH FONDANT

When you prepare a cake ready for painting, the technique that you follow is actually very similar to the process that you would follow when covering a cake in fondant using conventional cake-decorating methods. The biggest difference—and it is a crucial one—is that you must never use shortening (white vegetable fat) when rolling out your fondant because this will leave a greasy film on the surface, which will repel any colour that you paint onto it. For similar reasons, you must never use shortening to fill any cracks on the surface, and you must resist the temptation to add it to overly dry fondant. If your fondant does feel dry, or cracks when you roll it out, then you should add a teaspoon of glycerine (or even just a little cooled boiled water) and knead it into the fondant with your hands until the mixture attains the consistency you require.

If you normally use the mat technique to roll out your fondant, then you can continue to use this method as it will not affect the surface of the fondant. The mat technique uses two large sheets of food-grade plastic: you sandwich the fondant in between the sheets and roll it out. This means that you don't need to use any cornflour (cornstarch) and it can be easier to place the fondant on the cake.

If like me, you don't use a mat, use cornflour to roll out the fondant, or you may use icing (confectioners') sugar, but I personally find this can be a little bit too sticky to work with. Only use a sprinkling of cornflour, the minimum that you can get away with; if you use too much this will leave a layer of cornflour on the surface of your cake which can cause the colours to bleed when you apply them. (To make sure that your cake is ready for painting, run your hand over the fondant-covered cake—any grittiness you feel will be excess cornflour, which you can just rub away with your hand or paper towels.)

METHOD FOR COVERING THE CAKE WITH FONDANT

1   With a large flat brush, paint a thin layer of confectioners' glue or water onto the surface of the buttercream-covered cake (the buttercream should still be firm from being in the refrigerator). This is to give the fondant a sticky layer to adhere to and will help prevent tearing and air bubbles forming once the cake has been covered.

2   Knead the fondant until it becomes more pliable, but be careful not to overwork it, as this can make the fondant prone to tearing or cracking once it is on the cake.

Ease both hands under the fondant to lift

Place the fondant on the cake

Smooth the top

3   Sprinkle a fine layer of cornflour (cornstarch) onto the work surface and rub a little more onto the rolling pin. Place the fondant down and pat a small amount of the cornflour over the top.

4   Use spacers as a guide when you roll out the fondant. Keep turning the circle of fondant as you are rolling, to make sure it is not sticking to the work surface.

5   When the fondant has been rolled out, use a smoother to smooth out its surface until there are no bumps or indentations.

6   Slide your hands gently under the sheet of fondant. If you are covering a larger cake, then you may need to slide it further up your arms to support the fondant properly.

7   Carefully lift it onto the cake, positioning it centrally. Gently slide your hands out from beneath the surface.

8   With the palms of your hands, smooth the fondant down on the top of the cake, ensuring there are no air bubbles trapped underneath. If you do find any bubbles, just lift up the fondant to release them and smooth it down again. Use the palms of your hands to secure the fondant around the top edge of the cake—this is the area most likely to crack and tear, so be very gentle. When you are smoothing this area of the cake, work in an upwards direction (rather than pulling the fondant down over the edge of the cake) as this will help prevent any tearing. Then smooth down the sides of the cake, working your way around the circumference. If there are any folds of fondant at the bottom, lift up the skirt of fondant and push it in towards the bottom edge of the cake, unfolding any pleats as you do so. Repeat this technique all around the edge until you have a smooth surface with no folds.

9   Cut away the excess fondant with a sharp knife.

Smooth down the sides

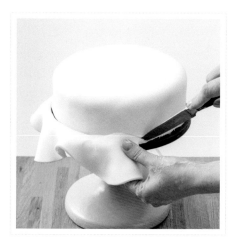

Cut away the excess

Use a smoother to finish

10 Use a smoother, and work it across the top and sides of the cake to create a flat and even finish.

11 Run the flat side of the cake scraper tool around the side of the cake, and use it to keep smoothing the fondant until the bottom edge of the cake is even and there are no cracks or gaps between the fondant and the board. There may be some excess fondant that needs to be cut at this point: if there is, then just smooth the edge again until you have achieved the required finish.

12 Once the cake is covered and the finish on the fondant is as perfect as you can make it (don't worry too much if there are a few flaws on the surface), leave it at room temperature in a dry place to firm up overnight. Never put a fondant-covered cake in the refrigerator or in an airtight box because this will cause it to sweat. If you need to keep it covered overnight, place it in a cupboard or a cardboard cake box. (See the section on storing cakes, page 86.)

COVERING A FRUIT CAKE

Fruit cakes have a naturally rougher texture than sponge, so I always cover my fruit cakes with marzipan before adding the fondant layer. But if you can't use marzipan because of taste or allergy issues, then use two layers of fondant instead. A second layer is essential, though—one layer of fondant is not enough to cover up the bumps and lumps in the cake caused by the fruit: so, the first layer is used as a substitute for the marzipan, and the second layer will have a much smoother finish.

I use sugar syrup to stick the marzipan layer on the cake, but I always make it with the alcohol that I have used in the cakes rather than with water.

METHOD FOR COVERING THE CAKE

1 If your cake has a slightly domed top, cut this off with a serrated knife to create a flat surface. Then turn the cake upside down and place it on a board which is at least 2"/50 mm bigger than the cake. Then put the cake (still on the board) onto a turntable.

2 Roll out small amounts of marzipan into long sausages and use these to fill any gaps at the bottom of the cake. Then use a cake scraper around the bottom edge, pressing it against the marzipan sausages to flatten them. This will create a nice flat surface along the side of the cake ready for covering.

3 Measure the circumference of the cake. Sprinkle the work surface with a fine layer of cornflour (cornstarch). Roll out half the remaining marzipan into a long strip using spacers—the length of this strip should be the same measurement as the circumference of the cake. Measure the height of the cake and trim the marzipan strip (along the long edge) until it matches your height measurement.

4 Brush the sugar syrup onto the sides of the cake and wrap the strip of marzipan around the edge.

5 Trim the marzipan where the two edges meet in order to create a smooth join.

6 Roll out the remaining marzipan into a circle to match the top of your cake, again using spacers to create an even surface.

7   Brush the top of the cake with sugar syrup and place the marzipan on top. Trim the edge with a sharp knife.

8   Use two smoothers to smooth down the marzipan. Try to create a sharp edge around the top of the cake.

9   Leave the marzipan-covered cake to stand overnight, so that the marzipan firms up.

10 The cake is then covered with fondant using the same method as described on pages 75–77 for a sponge cake. Brush the alcohol sugar syrup onto the marzipan to help the fondant stick to it, or you can use water or confectioners' glue.

Trim the top off the cake

Fill any gaps with marzipan

Smooth out the marzipan

Sprinkle cornflour on the surface

Make a marzipan strip

Brush the cake with sugar syrup

Cover the sides with marzipan

Trim the join

Smooth the join on the side

Lay the marzipan on top of the cake

Press down

Press along the join at the top

Trim away the excess

Smooth the marzipan

Cover the top and sides with syrup

Cover cupcake with buttercream

Place fondant circle on top of cupcake

Smooth fondant to a dome

COVERING CUPCAKES READY FOR PAINTING

I use two different methods to cover sponge cake cupcakes, depending on the style I want to achieve. The first method is to cover the entire top of the cake with a layer of fondant; the second is to pipe a buttercream swirl onto the cake and then top that with a painted fondant disc.

The first technique is really only suitable for very small quantities of painted cupcakes. Ideally I would suggest a batch of 12 and really no more than 36 (depending on the design). This is because such small covered cakes lose their freshness sooner than a large layered cake does. I normally bake cupcakes on the day they are going to be eaten or (at the very most) the day before. But this does not leave me much time to bake, then cover a large amount of cupcakes and paint them before they become stale. So, to circumvent this problem, the second "disc" method gives extra time to prepare toppers in advance, and I frequently use this technique when creating cupcake towers for weddings or events where there are hundreds of portions needed.

METHOD 1—FULLY COVERED CUPCAKES

1   Use a small offset spatula or a palette knife to create a mound of buttercream on top of the cupcake, then place it in the refrigerator for 15–20 minutes, until the buttercream is firm.

2   Knead the fondant briefly until it is pliable.

3   Sprinkle the work surface with a thin layer of cornflour (cornstarch) and roll out the fondant using spacers as guides.

4   Use a cutter that is ¾–1¼"/20–30 mm wider than the top of the cupcake to cut out circles in the fondant.

5   Place the fondant circle on top of the buttercream and smooth it down over the frosting. Use the palm of your hand to create an even dome. With the tip of your index finger, smooth the edge of the fondant so that it covers all the buttercream and there are no sharp edges.

6   When you cover large cakes or cookies, you need to leave the fondant to dry overnight before painting onto the surface—but cupcakes need to be eaten while still fresh, so only leave these to firm up for an hour (at the most) before painting.

Spooning buttercream into piping bag

Hold piping bag firmly at the top

Pipe the buttercream in a spiral motion

METHOD 2—CUPCAKES WITH FONDANT DISCS

1 At least two days before you will need to use the toppers, roll out modelling paste to a thickness of roughly 1/16"/2 mm. Cut circles out of the fondant using a cutter with a 2"/50 mm diameter (or thereabouts), and leave the toppers to dry (normally overnight). Once they are dry, you can paint them with your chosen design.

2 Place a large star-tipped nozzle in a piping (icing) bag, and then fill the bag two-thirds full with buttercream.

3 Hold the top of the piping bag firmly and pipe a small star of buttercream in the centre of the cake. This is to give the swirl you will create some height.

4 Starting at the edge of the cupcake, pipe in a spiral, moving towards the centre of the cake, building up around the star you first piped. At the top, release the pressure on the bag to form a point.

5 Wait until the last minute possible to place the toppers on the cupcakes: normally I do this at the venue once the cakes have been placed on their stand. This is because if there is too much heat or humidity, the toppers can melt or become floppy—and no one wants a floppy topper!

COVERING FRUIT CUPCAKES

1 Sprinkle the work surface with cornflour (cornstarch) and roll out the marzipan using spacers as guides to achieve an even thickness. Use a cutter that is the same size as the top of the cupcake to cut out circles in the marzipan.

2 Brush the surface of the cupcake with sugar syrup, place a marzipan circle on top of the cupcake and use the palm of your hand to smooth it down. Cover all the cupcakes in this manner.

3 Sprinkle your work surface with cornflour and roll out the fondant using the spacers as guides to achieve an even thickness. Use a cutter that is ¾–1¼"/20–30 mm larger than the top of the cupcake to cut out circles of the fondant.

4 Brush the marzipan with sugar syrup.

Finished buttercream swirl

Placing on the topper

Cupcake with fondant disc

5   Place the fondant circle on top of the marzipan and smooth it down. Use the palm of your hand to create an even dome. With the tip of your index finger, smooth the edge of the fondant so that it covers all the marzipan and there are no sharp edges.

COVERING COOKIES WITH FONDANT

Again, there are two slightly different methods that you can use to cover your cookies. If you need to make large amounts of cookies I recommend that you use a cookie cutter, even if you are intending to paint an unusual object or shape—you can place your chosen design in the centre of a circular or square cookie. For smaller quantities of cookies, you can hand-cut around a template, but this is quite time-consuming—which is why I would advise you to steer away from using this technique for batches of any more than, say 40 cookies.

METHOD USING A COOKIE CUTTER

1   Knead the fondant with your hands briefly until it is pliable.

2   Sprinkle the work surface with a thin layer of cornflour (cornstarch) and roll out the fondant using spacers as guides.

3   When the fondant is at the required depth, take a smoother and smooth the surface of the fondant until there are no bumps or indentations.

4   Use the same cutter that you used to make the cookies to cut out the required shape.

5   Paint a thin layer of confectioners' glue onto the cookie.

6   Place the cut-out fondant onto the cookie. Smooth it with the palm of your hand or a smoother.

7   If the cookie has spread slightly during cooking, there may be a gap between the edge and the edge of the fondant. You can cover this by very gently smoothing the fondant to the edge of the cookie, stretching it slightly to cover these gaps.

8   Leave the fondant-covered cookies in a cool dry place to firm up overnight before you start painting on them.

FONDANT-COVERED CUPCAKES

Brush the cupcake with sugar syrup

Place marzipan on top

Brush the marzipan with sugar syrup

Place the fondant over the marzipan

Smooth the edge with a finger

The fondant-covered cupcake

FONDANT-COVERED COOKIES

Applying confectioners' glue

Place the fondant on the cookie

The fondant-covered cookie

Cut out fondant using a template

Cut out dough using a template

Remove excess dough

METHOD USING A TEMPLATE

I normally use paper or card to create my template for this method, but if I have a large amount of cookies to cut out then I transfer the design onto a stiff food-grade plastic sheet. This is because paper can become greasy or wet when you cut around it (which can transfer dirt to the fondant), and it can also tear or break if used too many times. A plastic template can be washed so that you can use it to trace around both the cookies and the fondant without tearing.

1   Roll out the fondant using the method described on page 84.

2   Place the template on the fondant and cut around the edge using a scalpel or a sharp knife.

3   The rest of the technique is the same as described on page 84.

STORING FONDANT AND COVERED CAKES

Any leftover fondant you may have can be covered with plastic wrap and stored until needed. If it is going to be some time before you will be using it, then you can store it in the freezer, which will prevent it hardening. You can also store any modelling paste or leftover buttercream in this way.

Once your cake has been covered in fondant, you must still be very careful about storing it. Never put it in the refrigerator because, when you remove it, the fondant will start to sweat. It will also sweat if you store the cake in an airtight container—fondant-covered cakes are best kept in a container that will allow some airflow, and at room temperature (but be careful not to leave them too near a heat source or a window in full sun). So, if you want to cover them for storage, either leave them in a cupboard or use a cardboard cake box, which will allow the air to circulate.

Cupcake toppers made with modelling paste can be made and painted a few weeks in advance. Leave them out in the air until they have dried completely (if you have a spare cupboard you could leave them in that), then pack them carefully in a cardboard box, with parchment paper in between each layer. You can add a packet of silica gel to the box and this will absorb any moisture, but make sure it is properly sealed and that it doesn't touch the discs.

I appreciate that if you live in a very hot and humid place, storage outside a fridge may be problematic. Don't be concerned about your cakes or cookies going off if left out overnight. Cakes tend to go stale rather than off, but this can take over a week, and cookies will last for

up to a month. However, any buttercream underneath the fondant can soften slightly if it gets too hot and fondant can sweat if the humidity is too high, making it difficult to work on. If you have air conditioning, then this will keep your fondant perfect. De-humidifiers can also help to keep a cake in tip-top condition. (And, remember, you can leave the cake in a cardboard box with a packet of silica gel.)

If you don't have air conditioning, then you can add more icing (confectioners') sugar to your buttercream—if the buttercream is stiffer, it is less likely to bulge out of the layers. Of course, this will make it a lot sweeter, so try to strike a balance between making it thicker and still keeping it flavoursome.

If this doesn't work, then you can start painting on your cake as soon as you have covered it. But you must not use too much water as the fondant will get soggier more quickly, and be very careful not to lean on the cake or you will leave dents.

CREATING A TIERED CAKE

One of the most common questions that my students ask me is, "Do I put a tiered cake together and then paint it, or do I paint each tier separately and construct the cake later?" The answer is that I always merge the tiers first. This is because it is easier to paint the whole cake once it has been tiered so that there are no issues about lining up the design, and I can be sure that there are no gaps between tiers, helping to create a more pleasing finish (which saves having to cover up any problem areas with a ribbon).

Now, it is the cake decorator's worst nightmare to have a tiered cake collapse into a heap of nothing but cake crumbs (for me, in these terrifying dreams it always happens in a room full of guests in front of a horrified bride and groom). But banish these terrors from your mind! Merging together a tiered cake is actually quite simple. I admit that the idea can be daunting if you have never done it before, but just follow these simple steps and, instead of cries of horror, your perfectly balanced cake will invite gasps of amazement.

PREPARING CAKES FOR MERGING

1   The bottom tier of the cake can be placed on a covered ⅝"/15 mm cake drum as previously described. The other tiers of the cake also need to be supported by cake boards, no more than ¼"/4 mm deep (see the equipment list for details), but in a slightly different manner. The boards need to be the same width as the cakes, so place an 8"/200 mm cake on an 8"/200 mm board. These should not be the thick cake drums. It is best

Use a cake board as a guide

Insert one dowel to use as a measure

Use edible-paint pen to mark the length

to use 1/16–1/4"/2–4 mm thick boards which will not add too much height to the cake. Place the board under the cake at the filling stage, so that it becomes incorporated into the cake, and the fondant you apply will completely cover it. This means that when all the tiers are merged, you should not be able to see any of the boards at all. These boards will provide even support for the cake tier above.

2 Check at each stage (both when filling and covering the tiers with buttercream) that each cake is level: it is handy to have a small spirit level for this (but keep this purely for cake-decorating purposes, as you don't want brick dust in your cake). If the cake isn't level at any point, add some more buttercream to the lowest area and build it up. Then cover each tier with fondant and check the levels again. If, at this point, you find a tier that is uneven, then press down on the high side with a smoother to even it out.

METHOD FOR ADDING DOWELS TO THE CAKE

To support the tiers of the cake you will need to use dowels. These are available from cake-decorating suppliers, and can be plastic or wooden—either type will be perfectly suitable for these projects. Plastic dowels are either solid or hollow (which look like thick straws) and can be cut quite easily with a serrated knife, or even with scissors (but only the hollow types). Wooden dowels can be cut with wire cutters or a small hacksaw, so if you only have a knife or scissors to hand, go for one of the plastic types.

Dowels are only used to support the layer above them, so naturally the top tier will not need any. As a result I haven't given you the number of dowels needed in 4"/100 mm and 5"/130 mm cakes, as these are the smallest sizes and will always be the top tier.

A word of caution: do not, at any point, give in to your fears of a cake collapse and decide to insert more dowels than I have advised. Using too many will have the opposite effect—they will destroy the integrity of the cake's structure, and it will break into crumbs. It turns out that you *can* be too careful.

Number of dowels required for different cake sizes

Round cakes: 6"/150 mm – 3, 7"/180 mm – 4, 8"/200 mm – 4, 9"/230 mm – 5, 10"/250 mm – 5

Square cakes: 6"/150 mm – 4, 8"/200 mm – 4

Cut first dowel to size

Cut remaining dowels to size

Insert dowels into cake

METHOD FOR CUTTING DOWELS

1 Place the bottom tier of the cake on the covered cake board.

2 Take a cake board the same size as the next tier up, and gently press it into the centre of the top of the bottom tier. Lift it off carefully and you should be left with a faint impression of the cake board on the fondant. This will be your guide as to where you place the dowels so that they are hidden under the layer above and do not show.

3 Insert the first dowel into the cake, inside the guideline and relatively close to the edge—say, about ¼"/5 mm. Gently push it down so that it touches the board at the bottom. Use an edible paint pen to mark the point on the dowel where it exits the cake. Take this dowel out, and cut it to the height you have marked. Using this first dowel as a measure, cut the rest of the dowels for this tier to the same size.

4 Insert the dowels into the cake, making sure they are evenly spaced just inside the edge of the guidelines (in a circle or square). Repeat the steps for each tier.

METHODS FOR MERGING THE TIERS

There are two different approaches to create a merged cake.

The first is to cover all the tiers with fondant, then leave them to firm up overnight before merging them. This method will help to prevent you from making marks in the fondant when you are joining them, but the drawback is that you are more likely to end up with gaps between the layers. You can fix any gaps by carefully filling them with royal icing (mixed to the same colour as the fondant) or "let down" some of the fondant (this means adding water to a piece of fondant until it has a much softer consistency). You can then smooth the filler to create an even surface.

The other method is to cover each cake one at a time, and then immediately merge each of them in turn, adding each layer to the one below even before you cover the next in fondant. This obviously can lead to more marks on the fondant (because it is softer at the time you are working on it), but it helps to create a better fit between tiers.

The choice is really a personal one. I mostly use the second option so the cake is spending less time sitting around, and will be fresher.

Merging a tiered cake

You can use a few different methods to stick the tiers together—you can use a blob of royal icing, you can "let down" a small amount of the fondant until it becomes sticky and use this, or you can use some confectioners' glue.

1   Once the dowels have been inserted into the bottom layer, add the glue (or whatever you have chosen as your sticking solution) to the top of the cake, making sure that you keep it within the guideline of the upper tier.

2   Take the next tier: gently slide your hands under its board and carry it to the bottom tier (obviously the closer together the cakes are at this point, the less chance you have of dropping it). Carefully lower the second cake onto the one below, using the guidelines to position it centrally over the bottom tier. Lean the furthest part of the board onto the bottom tier and slide your hands out. The upper cake should only have a small way to fall until it settles on the bottom tier. Check that the second cake is placed centrally—if it is off-centre then gently (sooo gently . . .) push it from the side using an even pressure until the position is correct. You may need to re-smooth the side you pushed if it has any fingerprints.

3   Repeat the dowelling process for the second tier, then add the next tier on top in the same manner as described above. Continue dowelling until you have reached the final tier.

4   If you are merging the tiers fairly soon after they have been covered with fondant, you can then use your smoothers to make sure there are no gaps between layers. If the cakes are already too firm to do this, then fill in any gaps with royal icing or fondant.

MERGING A DOUBLE-BARREL CAKE

A double-barrel cake looks like a double-height cake—however, it is created by covering two cakes of the same size with one piece of fondant. This is so that the cake has more structural support, and also helps when you are cutting the cake, so that you do not end up with a long piece of cake! While merging the two tiers of the cake is relatively easy, covering them both with fondant is not. So, make sure that when you attempt this particular process, you are in a very calm state of mind—play some soothing music and drink chamomile tea.

The Cherry Blossom Cake (see page 119) is the only project in this book that requires a 5"/130 mm double-barrel cake, although it can also be made with three conventional tiers if you prefer.

1   Start with both the 5"/130 mm cakes sitting on 5"/130 mm cake boards, filled and covered with the crumb coat layer (see page 74).

2   Dowel one of the cakes with three dowels spaced evenly ¾"/20 mm in from the edge of the cake.

3   Place the cake without the dowels on top of the other one, making sure that the edges of the cakes line up.

4   Coat both the cakes with another crumb coat. Check the level of the cakes with a spirit level and add more buttercream to the lowest side if needed. Place the double-barrel cake in the refrigerator for 15–30 minutes. Take it out once the buttercream has hardened.

5   Roll out your fondant in the usual manner and place it over the cake.

6   The top of the cake is where you are likely to have the most difficulty. Because there is a long drop of fondant, it is easily pulled and torn. So, working quickly, press around the fondant on the top edge of the cake. Work your way down the side of the cake, but don't pull the fondant down.

7   You will find that there are more and bigger folds of fondant around the side of the cake than for a normal-sized cake. Gently unfold these and push the fondant back into the cake using the method described for a normal-sized cake (page 76).

8   Smooth, trim, and finish the cake using the method described for a normal-sized cake (see page 77).

9   If you have any small imperfections on the fondant, fill these with royal icing. Alternatively, you can "let down" some fondant, fill the tears, and then smooth over the area with a scraper. Make sure that this area is at the back of the cake.

— Chapter 5 —

Painting
Projects

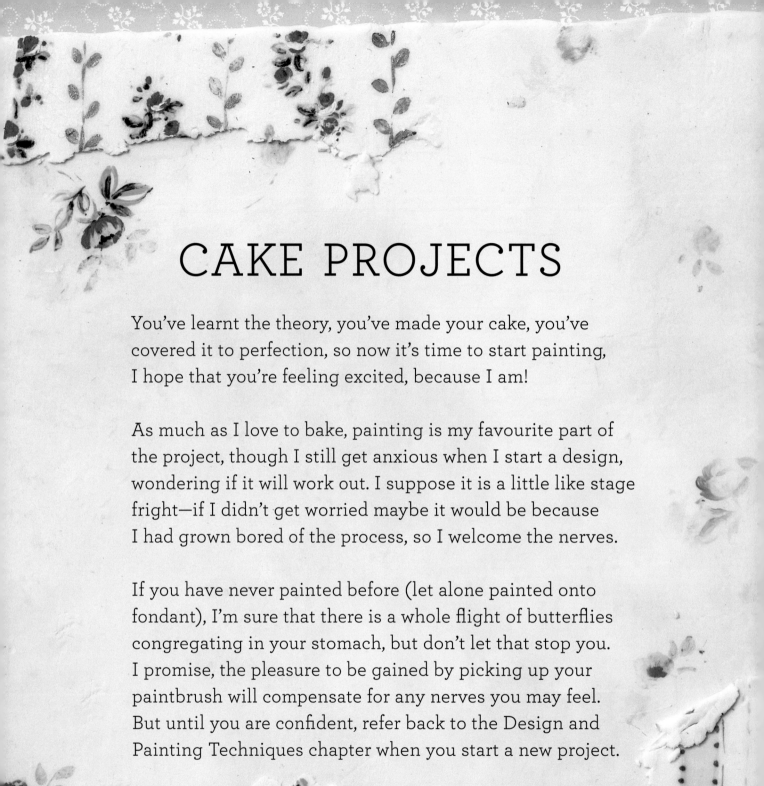

CAKE PROJECTS

You've learnt the theory, you've made your cake, you've
covered it to perfection, so now it's time to start painting,
I hope that you're feeling excited, because I am!

As much as I love to bake, painting is my favourite part of
the project, though I still get anxious when I start a design,
wondering if it will work out. I suppose it is a little like stage
fright—if I didn't get worried maybe it would be because
I had grown bored of the process, so I welcome the nerves.

If you have never painted before (let alone painted onto
fondant), I'm sure that there is a whole flight of butterflies
congregating in your stomach, but don't let that stop you.
I promise, the pleasure to be gained by picking up your
paintbrush will compensate for any nerves you may feel.
But until you are confident, refer back to the Design and
Painting Techniques chapter when you start a new project.

I have created some very easy projects for you to test the water with. Start with them and gradually work up to the more advanced projects. Once you are confident in your skills then it's time to go "off-piste." Mix up the projects—make a gold version of the rose cake, or add pansies to the trail cake—or why not make up a design that is totally your own. But for now it's time to dip your toe in (the water is warm, I promise you) and start painting. I can't wait to see what you create!

Key to projects
These indicate the level of difficulty involved in the painting of the project rather than in the covering and assembling of the cake.

Very easy ●

Easy ● ●

Medium ● ● ●

Hard ● ● ● ●

Advanced ● ● ● ● ●

MIMOSA BLOSSOM DESIGN

I created this for a friend's mimosa-themed baby shower. It is a really simple design, and incredibly easy to paint, so it's the perfect design for a beginner. The mimosa blossom is created with simple strokes for the stalks, and a series of blobs (that's my own highly technical term!) to represent the blossoms. This is a very forgiving design, too, so you can get away with some mistakes in your painting.

The trick to making this design look realistic is not to paint the elements too evenly—don't make the blobs too circular, and try to space them unevenly along the branch. Paint the lines for the branches with breaks and kinks, and, as with the blossoms, space the branches out unevenly around the cake. While it may sound counterintuitive to paint "unevenly" like this, it is the way to make something look more natural, and less like a stylised pattern.

I haven't created a topper to go with this cake, but it will need one. There are plenty of gorgeous ready-made toppers available from online craft sites, or you could add some fresh flowers. If you are adding flowers then make sure that they are not poisonous, and cut a little circle of food-grade cellophane to place under the flowers, as this will stop any water affecting the fondant.

EQUIPMENT

Paintbrushes, sizes 4, 0

Colours

Yellow, orange, brown

A 6"/150 mm cake covered in white fondant

1. Paint a series of yellow blobs with the size 4 brush to create the mimosa blossom. You don't want to make perfectly round circles, so make sure they are all slightly different shapes—"blobby" is good. Make sure to keep the blossoms uneven, with a few of the blobs together at the top, then perhaps two on one side, and on the opposite side of what will eventually be the stem, one blossom on its own or maybe a bunch of three together.

2. Add a dab of orange on each yellow blossom. Don't worry if the colours bleed together a little, this will only add to the effect. However, if you find the colours are actually running down the cake, then your brush is too wet.

3. Use the size 0 brush with neat brown to paint the stalks. Try to keep the brushstrokes as light as possible. Give each stalk a slightly different angle and make sure that they are not too straight. By adding breaks in the stalk you make it more realistic—you don't want to create heavy marks that have no movement

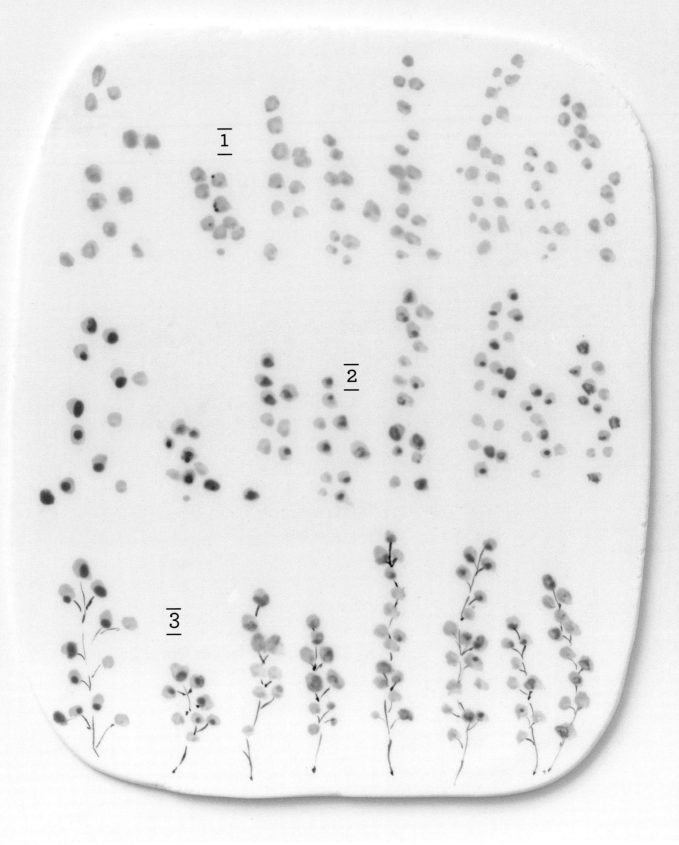

BOLD OUTLINE CAKE

This may come as a shock, but not everyone appreciates a pretty floral cake (I know—it's unbelievable, right?). And while I can never sate my appetite for blousy roses, I do also love more modern, striking designs.

This project is very easy to paint—and has a really big impact. You can change the colour palette to create a totally different effect, but I like the "Great Gatsbyesque" feel of the black, gold and grey. The Cake Gatsby, if you will . . .

EQUIPMENT

Paintbrush, size 4

Tracing paper

Non-toxic pencil

Colours

Black, metallic gold

An 8"/200 mm cake covered in a medium tone of grey fondant

1   Enlarge the template *(Template 1, page 224)* by 145%, then trace onto tracing paper. Trace the flowers in a pattern all over the cake, making sure that they are evenly spaced and that there is enough space in between them to add the spots.

2   Paint the centre of the flowers and the spots in between them with the metallic gold. You may need to apply two coats to ensure an even coverage, but make sure that the first coat is completely dry before you add the second.

3   Once the gold is dry, paint the outline of the flowers in black.

LACE DESIGN

When my husband and I celebrated joint special birthdays (we both turned 21 . . . again!), I asked him what his preference would be for the party decorations. His response was to look at me like I had suggested that we hire an elephant and fly it to the moon; it's safe to say the idea of party decorations mattering in the slightest hadn't even entered his head.

So I spent some time enlightening him on the desperate need to have a theme and a colour palette, or our big bash would be an uncoordinated disaster. He couldn't quite seem to grasp that this mattered that much, but I finally pushed him into an opinion, which was "Nothing too girly." (He knew from past experience that there was a high likelihood I would fill the hall with pink roses and glitter.)

Finding a theme to satisfy the two of us and leave me with enough time to shop for a new dress and shoes and have my hair styled was certainly easier said than done! However, I love a challenge. Eventually I settled on a green, grey, and silver theme, with moss and ferns decorating the tables. I created three smaller cakes for a dessert table, matching my colour theme, and this lace cake was one of them.

You can use any lace impression mat or mould that you can find. Preferably it should have one edge that is scalloped or shaped in an interesting way, but the opposite edge is not as important as it will be cut straight along the edge of the cake. Obviously it would be very easy for you to change the feel of this design by experimenting with the colours or adding a different topper.

EQUIPMENT

Paintbrush, size 4, and a brush for gluing

7 oz/200 g modelling paste

Confectioners' glue

Tracing paper

Non-toxic pencil

Scalpel

Extruder

Lace mat

Colours

Grey, black

A 6"/150 mm cake covered in ivory fondant. You'll need a slightly taller cake than normal: it should be about 4"/100 mm tall

1 Colour the modelling paste light grey—add a small amount of colour at a time, and knead well until you have the correct tone.

2 Reserve a little paste to use as a seal. Roll out half the remaining modelling paste into a thin ribbon that is long enough to reach all the way around the cake. Put the lace mat on top of the paste and press down firmly, then remove it. If you cannot see the pattern of the lace clearly enough, you will need to start again from the beginning—it's not worth trying to line the mat up again on the pattern you've made to try and make a deeper impression.

3 Carefully cut around the scalloped edge of the pattern using a scalpel, and then cut the opposite edge in a neat straight line.

4 Brush glue around the top edge of the side of the cake, and stick the lace ribbon of paste onto the cake, aligning the straight edge of your cut-out with the top of the cake. Make sure that you join up the two ends of the ribbon at the back of the cake, then trim off any excess.

Cut around the scalloped edge of the lace

Glue the ribbon of paste to the cake

Extrude a length of paste to seal the join

5   Brush a thin line of glue around the top of the ribbon of paste.

6   "Let down" a small amount of the grey modelling paste (this means mix a little water into it until it becomes less stiff). Then, using a medium round hole on the extruder, extrude a length of the grey paste around the top of the cake, keeping the join at the back.

7   Repeat the above process for the second strip of lace, sticking it to the bottom edge of the cake, and glue a length of the extruded modelling paste at the base of the lace.

8   Trace the template design (*Template 2, page 224*) onto tracing paper, then transfer the pattern to run around the centre of the side of the cake. You may need to either add some longer stalks, or even make them shorter so that the design fits neatly around the cake.

9   Use the size 4 paintbrush to paint the flowers, leaves and stalks in a pale grey.

10   Use a neat grey to add definition and shadow to the flowers and leaves.

11   Mix together a small amount of the grey and black to use in the very centre of the flowers, and a little touch on some of the leaves.

12   Finish the cake off with oodles of candles—although if this reminder of their increasing years might distress the recipient of the cake, then perhaps add fresh flowers instead (making sure they are not poisonous), or an alternative topper.

SINGLE ROSE CAKE

This is such a simple design to recreate: a single flower repeated over the whole cake. For this project I have used a rose, but you could easily substitute another flower. Daisies, pansies, or hydrangeas would all work just as well—what I'm really trying to say is that you can use any flower you want! I've used yellow tones in this cake. Of course, you can paint it in different colours if you wish, but I love this bright, sunny colour palette.

EQUIPMENT

Paintbrush, size 8, and a size 4 (optional)

Tracing paper

Non-toxic pencil

Colours

Yellow, soft green, orange, white, dark green, pink

A 6"/150 mm cake covered in pale yellow fondant

1 Using the template (*Template 3, page 224*), trace the outline of the rose and leaves from the template provided, and transfer the design to the cake. Make sure the flowers are evenly spaced around the cake, and that they are pointing in different directions, rather than all facing the same way.

2 Using the yellow paint and the size 8 brush, paint in the roses, remembering to leave some areas free from paint. (You will find that it is more difficult to create a difference in tones when using yellow because it is such a light colour, but do not worry too much as you'll later apply orange and pink to create darker tones.)

3 Paint the leaves with a light tone of soft green. Again, leave some areas of each unpainted. If you have any slight gaps in your layout you can always add a few extra leaves at this point.

4 Add detail to the roses with a medium tone of orange.

5 Add a second layer of neat orange.

6 Add some highlights to the flowers and leaves with white.

7 Add shading to the leaves with neat soft green.

8 Add some extra shading to the leaves with neat dark green.

9 Paint the final layer of shadow in the centre of the rose with neat pink. If you wish, you can add some pink detail onto a few of the leaves (just don't add it to each and every one). You can also add some pink dots to your design—you may wish to change to the size 4 brush for this.

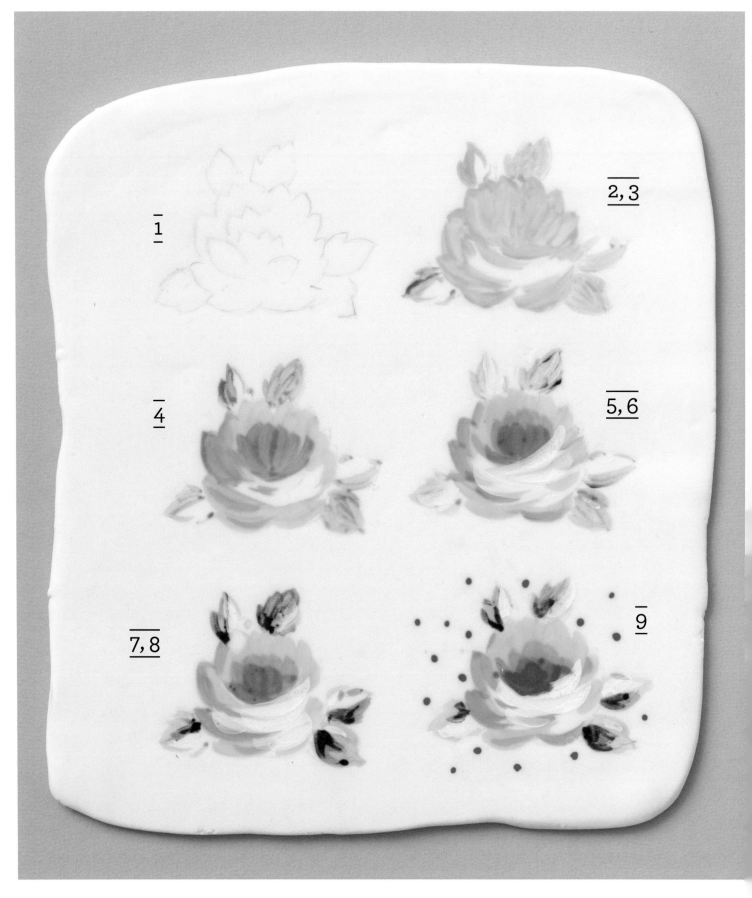

WOODLAND CAKE

One of my children (who shall remain nameless, but she knows who she is!) has an all-consuming obsession with owls. This passion started after a visit to an owl sanctuary that coincided with us reading Jill Tomlinson's *The Owl Who Was Afraid of the Dark* together. Since then, the house has been filled with a full parliament of stuffed toy owls, and she refuses to wear any clothes that don't feature her bird of choice. I rather suspect she would eat mice if she could.

Every year I make my family a painted gingerbread house, and the year that her obsession started there was a request for one with an owl theme. I created a set of bird-house cakes with various owls roosting in them, giving them a slight "vintage print" feel by using basic patterns with a restricted palette.

I really wanted to create a project for you based on these gingerbread houses, so I have replaced the bird house with a lovely tree for the owl to roost in. I also felt he may be a little lonely on his own, so I have given him some woodland friends to keep him company. I think my owl-fancier would approve.

This design would be easy to replicate on a smaller cake or even a round cake. Just reduce the template of the tree and bushes so that they fit onto the top of your chosen cake.

EQUIPMENT

Paintbrushes, sizes 8, 4, 0, and a brush for gluing

5½ oz/150 g modelling paste

Confectioners' glue

Tracing paper

Non-toxic pencil

Scalpel

Foam mat

6"/150 mm lollipop sticks

Cocktail sticks (optional)

Colours

Brown, pink, soft green, brown, blue

An 8"/200 mm square cake covered in white fondant

1 **Method for the tree plaque** *(illustrated on page 114)*

a Roll out the modelling paste to an even thickness of ¼"/4–5 mm. Ball up the remaining paste and leave it wrapped in cling film to keep it from drying out before you need to use it again.

b Enlarge the template *(Template 4, page 225)* by 120% and trace the outline of the plaque onto the rolled-out modelling paste. You don't need to trace every element of the design, just the main outlines: the tree trunk and branches, the outline of the bush, and the owl. The other, smaller elements are such simple shapes that you can paint them directly onto the plaque. If you do this your colours will have more clarity as they will not be mixed with pencil lines.

c Cut out the plaque using a scalpel.

d Use a light tone of brown with the size 8 brush to paint the tree trunk and branches.

e Switch to the size 4 brush and use a light tone of pink to paint the outer part of the body of the owl and the flowers on the bush.

f Paint the rest of the owl with a light tone of soft green, then add in the leaves.

g When the first layer of colour is dry, switch to a size 0 brush and paint the outlines and the dots that run up the side of the tree trunk in dark brown.

Glue the fondant over the stick

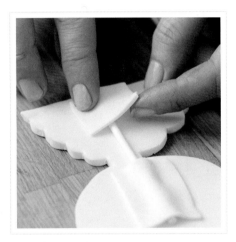

Press down gently

Back of the finished plaque

h   Paint blue dots around the leaves of the tree. Leave the plaque to firm up on a foam mat.

i   Once the plaque is firm and the paint has dried, turn it over. Place the lollipop stick on the back, right in the middle of the design— making especially sure that it runs along the middle of the tree trunk where it is at its thinnest, as this is where the plaque is most likely to break. Glue two rectangles (½ x 1¼"/10 x 30 mm) of modelling paste over the stick. Leave the plaque face down until the glue has completely dried.

2   Method for the two smaller plaques *(illustrated on page 114)*

a   Roll out the modelling paste to an even thickness of ¼"/4–5 mm.

b   Enlarge the templates *(Templates 5 and 6, page 225)* by 120% and trace the outline of the two smaller plaques onto the rolled-out modelling paste. Again, don't trace the small elements of the design, just the main outlines.

c   Cut out the plaques.

d   Paint the flowers using light tones of blue or pink.

e   Paint the fox and the hedgehog using a light brown tone.

f   Wash off any pencil marks left around the outline of the bushes, then paint the leaves and the dots around the bushes using a light tone of soft green.

g   Outline the animals and leaves using neat brown with a size 0 brush. Leave these two plaques to firm up on a foam mat.

3   Method for painting the sides of the cakes *(illustrated on page 114)*

a   Draw the outline of the trail using soft green with the size 0 brush. The trail should have lots of branches which are all very circular in shape. Make sure that part of the trail reaches the bottom edge of the cake and looks as if it goes beyond that point. Ensure that you don't end up with a white line around the bottom of the cake.

b   Switch to the size 4 brush, then paint in the leaves using a medium tone of soft green.

c   Paint the blue flowers at the end of each of the branches. If you have any gaps in the design, you can always add a floating flower or two to fill them in. Paint a pink dot in the centre of each flower.

d   Outline the leaves with neat brown, using the size 0 brush.

Form the fondant into a cone

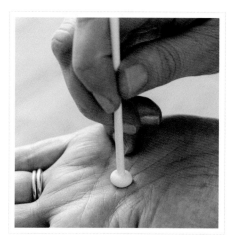

Make an indent in the ball

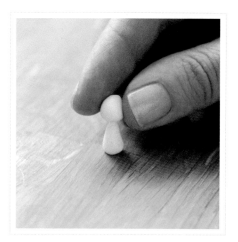

Glue the mushroom together

4 Method for making mini fondant mushrooms

a Take a tiny piece of fondant, roughly ⅜ x ¹⁄₁₆"/7 x 2 mm in size. Using the tips of your fingers, roll it into a sausage shape. Then push one end onto a flat surface as you twirl the other end in between your thumb and first finger. This will create a cone shape, the base of your mushroom.

b Take a similar sized piece of fondant and roll it into a ball. Push the end of a lollipop stick into one side of the ball and, with your fingers, mould the sides of the ball around the stick. This will form the top of the mushroom.

c Glue the top of the mushroom onto the top of the cone.

d You can change the shape and size of all your mushrooms, but don't make them too large as their charm lies in their smallness.

5 Once the plaques are dried, place them onto the cake. Be careful with the tree plaque—you may find it helpful to create a hole in the cake using a spare lollipop stick first. You should be able to glue the small plaques straight onto the cake, but if you find this difficult (normally because the bottom edge isn't completely straight or you have rolled out the modelling paste too thinly), then you can glue a cocktail stick to the back of them and support them in that way.

6 Glue the mushrooms on the top of the cake (you can also add a few to the cake board if you wish).

CHRISTMAS CAKE

Much as I love baking, I know from experience that, come Christmas time—having spent all of Stir-up Sunday baking a delicious rich Christmas cake, and then diligently feeding it with brandy for the next few weeks—I really do not want to spend any more of my time than is necessary trapped in my kitchen wrestling with fondant. At the festive time of the year there are always presents to wrap, cards to write and parties to attend, and so this is the perfect design for an easy, fun and, best of all, quick family Christmas cake. It is simple enough for your kids to make, leaving you enough time to perfect your eggnog recipe (or just to catch up on some sleep!).

I suggest you use a 6"/150 mm cake, but you can make your cake any size you need, depending on how many you will be feeding on Christmas Day. Just enlarge the template until the design fits comfortably on top of your cake.

EQUIPMENT
Paintbrushes, sizes 8, 4, 0, and size 8 for gluing

3½ oz/100 g modelling paste

Confectioners' glue

Tracing paper

Non-toxic pencil

Scalpel

Small white snowflake sprinkles (or white nonpareils)

Ribbon

Colours
Blue, red, yellow, white, brown

A 6"/150 mm cake covered in white fondant

1 Roll out the modelling paste to a thickness of 1/16"/2 mm. Using the non-toxic pencil, trace around the template (*Template 7, page 226*), then cut it out with a scalpel to create the snow globe. Paint glue onto the back of the shape and paste it onto the top of the cake.

2 Use the size 8 brush to paint a pale tone of blue to create shadow on the snowman and the banner. Paint the hat and the scarf with neat yellow. With a medium tone of red, paint the base of the snow globe. Mix together some red and yellow to create an orange tone and paint the carrot nose with the size 4 brush. Mix together a small amount of red with white to create a pale pink, and use this to paint the snowman's rosy cheeks.

3 With the size 8 brush, add white highlights to the hat and one side of the base.

4 Add neat red shading on the other side of the base. Switch to the size 0 brush and use the neat red to paint a message on the banner, the spots on both the hat and scarf, and also the tassels on the scarf.

5 With the size 0 brush, use neat brown to paint the outlines. This does not need to be a continuous line—it will actually improve the appearance if there are breaks and differences in the thickness of the lines.

6 Glue the sprinkles onto the snow globe.

7 Use the size 0 brush with a medium tone of blue to paint the stars on the top of the cake.

8 Finish by tying a ribbon around the side, with a lovely big bow at the front.

CHERRY BLOSSOM CAKE

I spend an awful lot of time trawling the internet looking at decorated cakes (it's a hard job, but somebody has to do it). One style that I have often admired is where the decorator has moulded a branch of cherry blossom across the cake, so I decided to create my own painted version. Because the cherry blossom is only painted on the front of the cake, this is a really quick design to execute. You can add a few little flowers to dance around the side of the cake if you wish, just to add some more interest (or, if you are like me, to cover up small imperfections in the fondant).

I have used a double-barrel cake (two 5"/ 130 mm cakes merged together and covered with one sheet of fondant, see pages 90–91) for the top tier. I'm not going to pull the wool over your eyes here—this is a particularly tricky technique to master, so if the thought of covering a cake like this is too daunting for you, then by all means recreate this cake using three normal tiers.

EQUIPMENT

Paintbrushes, sizes 4, 0
Colours
Pink, white, yellow, soft green, brown
A two-tiered cake consisting of a 7"/180 mm cake and a double-barrel 5"/130 mm cake, covered with white fondant (or a three-tiered cake with 8"/200 mm, 6"/150 mm and 4"/100 mm layers)

1   Sketch the basic structure of the branches onto the fondant (see page 120) by painting with a very pale tone of brown or drawing with a non-toxic pencil.

2   Mix up a pale tone of pink and paint in the blossoms with the size 4 brush. Each flower consists of five rounded petals. Leave the centre of each flower free of paint, so that when you add the yellow it doesn't become muddy. You can add some blossoms that are painted to look as if you are viewing them from the side—they will have two or three petals and a small blob of green at their base to indicate the receptacle of the flower.

3   Mix up a medium tone of pink and add some shading to the blossoms. Add some white highlights to the blossoms.

4   Paint a small circle of yellow in the centre of each flower.

5   Paint in the leaves using a pale tone of soft green. You can also add some stalks to some of the flowers and leaves, but use the size 0 brush for these to create a nice thin line, and don't forget to add the receptacles.

6   Add shading and other details to the leaves using neat soft green.

7   Paint the branches using a medium tone of brown.

8   Add shading onto the branches with neat brown.

9   Again using neat brown but with the size 0 brush, paint small dots around the yellow flower centres.

BASIC ROSE CAKE

This is the first design I created to teach to a class. Roses were an obvious choice as most of my students want to learn how to paint them, and I have painted very few wedding cakes that don't contain a rose or two as part of the design. When you master this design, you will have learnt the foundations for creating two different versions of a gorgeous rose.

The first rose is painted as if you are looking at it from the side, giving a view onto its gorgeous blousy petals, and the other gives the impression that we are looking straight down onto its centre.

The trick to perfecting a beautiful rose is to create a real difference in the tonal value of the colours. In the rose, there should be a very light pink or white tone for the highlights, graduating to a much darker tone for the shadows and the centre. The most common problem I see when first-time artists are painting roses onto fondant is in the flatness of the painting—there isn't enough variation in tone across each flower. This is easily avoided; if you make sure that the centre of the flower is at least three tones darker than the lightest point, your painting will look wonderful.

EQUIPMENT

Paintbrushes, sizes 8, 4

Tracing paper

Non-toxic pencil

Colours

Pink, blue, purple,

soft green, bright green,

white, green, yellow,

dark brown

An 8"/200 mm cake covered in white fondant

1 Use a very pale tone of brown to roughly sketch out the layout of the design onto your cake. Each group of flowers that you are going to paint will ultimately consist of two roses, a cluster of forget-me-nots and some leaves, but only sketch out circles to indicate the rose flowers at this point. You will add the leaves to the design after painting in the flowers. This is because the leaves are perfect for filling gaps and spaces in the layout, and by leaving them until last it will help you to achieve a better overall design. So make sure that there is an even amount of space around each individual group to leave enough room for the leaves; I normally allow about a 2"/ 50 mm gap. Once you have finished the rough sketch, use the templates and tracing paper to transfer the outline of the flowers. Enlarge the templates (*Templates 8–12, page 228*) by 140%.

2 Mix up a very pale pink tone and use your size 8 brush to create the petals of the first rose (this is the rose with a side-on view). Add some leaves around this flower in soft green, and then use a darker tone of pink to create the first layer of colour for the second rose (this is the rose that is viewed straight-on). Use light tones of blue and purple to paint the first layer of forget-me-nots. Each forget-me-not is created by painting five round petals, noting that the petals of each flower should not meet in the middle to leave enough space for the yellow centre. Some of the forget-me-not petals

should be painted to give the appearance that they are behind the rose or the leaves. Be careful not to leave a gap between the rose and the forget-me-nots as this will look unnatural. To complete this layer, fill in the rest of the leaves using light tones of soft green and bright green.

3   Now mix up a slightly darker tone of pink, and work it into the centre of the first rose. Add some darker pink to one side of the flower to create the effect of shadow. Then use another, darker tone of pink for the next layer of the second rose, again focusing on the centre and the darkest part of the bloom—this will be at the point where this rose emerges from underneath the first, and where there are leaves on top. Add some neat blue and purple to a few of the forget-me-not petals. Paint additional detail onto the leaves in the neat soft green, remembering to paint in the direction of the leaf veins (as described in the Design and Painting Techniques chapter, page 41).

4   On the light side of the first rose, add a few strokes of white (but don't go overboard). You can also add some highlights of the white onto the leaves and forget-me-nots. With neat pink, add more definition to the centres of the roses. On a few of the leaves, paint in extra details with neat dark green. Add a dot of yellow in the centre of each forget-me-not.

5   Once the paint from the previous stage has dried to a slight tackiness, add neat brown to the very centre of the roses and a few strokes on the leaves. If you wish, you can add a little neat pink to the sides of some of the rose leaves. Finally, with the size 4 brush, paint little dots of neat purple onto the end of the petals of the forget-me-nots.

BUNTING CAKE WITH TOPPER

The bunting cake is easy to make, as painting elements first and then sticking them onto a cake should take away any stress—you don't have to get the painting right first time. If you paint a flag that you aren't happy with, you can easily start again and make a better one.

If you are nervous about painting, you can print patterns onto icing and cut those down into flags. If you don't have an icing printer, you may find someone local who has the facilities for edible printing. If not, there are businesses on the internet who offer this service. You can also buy ready-made printed icing sheets from cake-decorating suppliers.

It's easy to incorporate a message—you can write each letter of the message onto its own flag of the bunting, or you could use the stamp method which is described in the Cheats section (page 206).

Here's the trick for painting very small elements: keep it simple! Do not try and add too much detail, or too many layers of shading, or the elements can become fussy and you can lose definition.

I have included the method for making number toppers, perfect for a birthday or anniversary. You can use the templates or make your own. I suggest you use a chunky font, otherwise the numbers may be too spindly and break easily. If you do want a more delicate typeface, add more space around it, or paint the negative space around the letter. Of course, this design is very easy to change for different recipients by varying the colours or patterns.

EQUIPMENT

Paintbrushes, sizes 4, 0, and a brush for gluing

6½"/180 g modelling paste

Confectioners' glue

Tracing paper

Non-toxic pencil

Scalpel

Foam mat

Extruder

Lollipop sticks

Cocktail stick

Tape measure

Colours

Yellow, orange, pink, dusky pink, blue, white, soft green, dark green, brown

A 7"/180 mm cake covered in white fondant

Method for making the bunting

The bunting is made up of small triangular flags. There are five swags around the cake and each swag should be long enough for five flags. Because the circumference of a cake can vary depending on how thick you make your crumb coat (the layer of buttercream underneath the fondant), or how thinly you roll out your fondant, you may need to increase or decrease the space between each flag.

1 Take four ¼ oz/10 g balls of the modelling paste and colour one ball in light pink, one in light blue and one in light orange. Keep the last one white.

2 Roll each colour out, one at a time, to a thickness of ¹⁄₃₂"/1 mm. Cut out seven flags from each colour using the template (*Template 13, page 228*). You will need a few extra in each of the four colours in case there are any breakages.

3 Paint the rose bunting using the following method:
a Take seven flags in a mix of colours. Paint small circles in groups of three onto the flags, using a medium tone of pink with the size 4 brush.
b Add small strokes of white onto the circles.
c Use neat pink to add depth to the centre of each circle. You can add ⟹

Cake projects 127

a little onto some of the edges of the circles (but don't add it to every one).

d   Add some leaves using soft green.

4   Paint the gingham-patterned bunting using the following method:

a   Choose six flags in a mix of colours. Use a light tone that is the same colour as the flag for the first layer of colour—so if you have a pink flag, use light pink paint, and use light blue paint for the blue flag, etc. Use any colour you wish for the white flags.

b   Paint vertical lines onto the flags with your chosen colour and the size 4 brush. Make the painted lines the same width as the gaps between them.

c   Paint horizontal lines using the same method.

d   Paint squares where the two solid lines cross each other, using the neat tone of your chosen colour.

5   Paint the polka dot daisy bunting using the following method:

a   Choose six flags in a mix of colours. Paint daisies in a polka dot pattern on to each of the flags using the size 4 brush and white paint. You can use any colour you like for the white flags.

b   Add a dot of orange in the centre of each daisy on the coloured flags (but a different colour if you have used orange for the petals on the white flag).

6   Paint the blue flower-patterned bunting using the following method:

a   Choose six flags in a mix of colours. Paint the five petals of the flower using a medium tone of blue. Take care to centre the flower on the flag and leave the middle of the flower unpainted.

b   Paint the leaves around the flower with a light tone of green.

c   Paint some shading onto the petals of the flower with neat blue.

d   Paint some shading onto the leaves using neat green.

e   Paint a white dot in the centre of the flower and add some small white dots around the flag. If the flag is white, use a different colour for the centres.

7   Measure the circumference of your cake and divide it by five. Then mark out each fifth on the top with the cocktail stick. This will give you the measurement for each swag of the bunting.

8   Extrude a thin white string of fondant and glue it around the cake in swags, finishing the top of each swag at the marks you have made, so each swag should be of equal length. (If you have ninja-level piping skills, you can simply pipe the string.)

9   Glue the flags to the cake, placing the top of each flag under the string. There should be five flags to each swag. Take care that you don't create a repeating pattern—try to deliberately have two flags of the same colour next to each other at various points, or two that have the same pattern.

Method for making the number toppers

When painting a figure such as a number or letter that is to be patterned with a ditsy print, imagine that the figure has been cut out of fabric, and the edge of the figure has small details of flowers or leaves cut off from the rest of its body. Make sure you don't end up with an unpainted gap around the edge of the figure (although you need an empty border around the outer edge to define the shape). If you decide to paint the negative space around the number, the reverse is true: the pattern should appear to go over the edge of the fondant.

1   Roll out the remaining white modelling paste to a thickness of ¼"/5 mm. Cut out the figures you require using the templates, adding a border of ¼"/5 mm around each number (enlarge *Templates 14 and 15, page 228*, by 165%, and *Templates 16–23, page 230*, by 133%).

2   With a non-toxic pencil, draw the number on the fondant topper.

3   **For the first number**

a   Use a light tone of pink and the size 4 brush to paint ⟹

3a

3b, c

3d

4a

4b

4c

in the roses and then switch to a pale tone of soft green to paint in the leaves.

b   Add neat pink to show the shading on the roses, and neat green shading on the leaves.

c   Mix together some pink and white to create a pale pastel pink. Use this colour to paint the background of the figure (leaving the white border). Leave some small circles of unpainted white in the background, but don't worry if you can't see these too well and they don't really stand out, because you will outline them next.

d   When the previous layers are totally dry, use the size 0 brush to paint an outline on the flowers, the leaves, and the white circles with neat brown. Use the same colour to outline the number.

e   Leave the topper to dry on a foam mat.

4   For the second number *(if you need one)*

a   Paint the pink roses with a light tone and use the size 4 brush. Use a light tone for the orange flowers and a light tone of soft green for the leaves and stalks (you may need to switch to a size 0 brush for the stalks in order to get them really thin).

b   Paint a medium-to-dark tone of pink in the centre of the pink flowers, a neat tone of orange in the centre of the orange flowers, and a neat soft green shading on the leaves.

c   Once the previous layers are completely dry, outline all the flowers and leaves with neat blue, using a size 0 brush. Outline the number in the same way.

d   Leave the topper to dry on a foam mat.

5   When both the toppers are firm, turn them over. Place a lollipop stick on the back of each one (this

may not necessarily be in the middle of the topper, but should be in a place where it won't be seen from the front—so on the number 4, it will be behind the leg). Glue three rectangles of modelling paste (1/2 x 3/4"/10 x 20 mm) over each stick to hold it in place. Leave the toppers lying face down until the glue has completely dried.

6   Carefully place the numbers on the top of the cake. You may find it easier to make a hole with a spare lollipop stick first—this is so that you don't put too much pressure on the toppers, avoiding the risk of having them break.

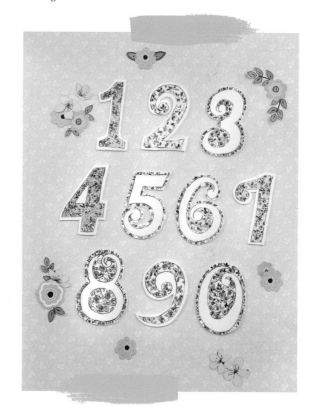

BLUE TRAIL CAKE WITH BUTTERFLIES ● ● ● ●

This is a really pretty and delicate cake, perfect for an afternoon tea with the girls or for a special birthday. And if you want to create an amazing wedding cake, you can simply use the same basic pattern but increase the number of tiers to result in a more dramatic cake.

The bottom tier is painted with a trailing design, where sprigs of flowers spring from a main stalk which curls around the cake. Over an 8"/200 mm cake you should be able to paint four main branches of the trail. These don't all need to grow from the base of the cake; some can sprout from the top of the cake (where it meets the next tier) and grow downwards. Every stalk should be curved, rather than being too straight (which would make your design look stilted and clumsy). If you have any gaps left on this tier once you have finished painting the trail add a floating flower or a sprig of leaves.

This project also teaches you how to paint 3D butterflies, which can be added to any of the projects in this book if you have the inclination, or you could even create a cake made up solely of a flight of butterflies. (The other collective noun for butterflies is a "rabble," but I'm sure that your cake would in no way deserve that description!) Don't worry if your butterfly cutters are a different shape from the ones I have used: you may need to change the painted design slightly but they will still look fabulous.

EQUIPMENT

Paintbrushes, sizes 4, 0, and a brush for gluing

1 oz/30 g modelling paste

Confectioners' glue

Butterfly-shaped cookie cutters, one with wingspan of about 2½"/60 mm, one with wingspan of about 1½"/40 mm

Cardboard

Colours

Pink, yellow, white, soft green, dark green, blue, purple, orange, brown

A two-tiered cake consisting of an 8"/200 mm cake and a 6"/150 mm cake, covered in white fondant

1 Method for creating the butterflies *(illustrated on page 134)*

a   Roll out the modelling paste to a thickness of $^1/_{32}$"/1mm or less.

b   Cut out three large butterflies and one small one (and I always make a few extra in case of breakages, as they can be so delicate).

c   Fold a strip of card in half. Gently fold two of the large butterflies and place on the fold of the card (add an extra one or two in case of breakages). They will dry in the shape of a resting butterfly.

d   Place the remaining butterflies on a square of parchment paper. Gently push the edge of the wings towards each other so the middle of the wings are slightly raised, then leave the butterflies in this position to harden overnight.

2 Method for painting the first butterfly *(illustrated on page 135)*

a   Mix up a light tone of blue and paint in the blue detail on the wings using the size 4 brush. Allow each layer of colour to dry completely before adding the next colour (something you should do for every step).

b   Mix up a medium tone of brown, then paint in the body of the butterfly and the decorative details.

c   Use neat brown to add shading to the body and final detailing on the wings.

3 Method for painting the second butterfly *(illustrated on page 135)*

a   Paint the middle half of the wings with yellow, then use a medium tone of blue to colour the remaining area of the wings. ⟹

Place the butterflies on folded card

Leave to dry

Gently push wings to create the shape

b   Paint the body of the butterfly with orange and add some orange detail on the wings.

c   Use neat brown to add shading and detail to the body and wings.

4   **Method for painting the third butterfly**

a   Use yellow to paint the top half of the upper wings and the end tips of the bottom wings. Fill in the rest of the wings with orange.

b   Paint the body of the butterfly with a light tone of brown and add some shading and detail on the wings.

c   Use neat brown to add shading and detail to the wings and body.

5   **Method for painting the fourth butterfly** *(the smallest one)*

a   Use a light tone of blue to paint a circle on each of the upper wings. Then paint a horseshoe shape on each of the lower wings. Paint the rest of the wings using a light tone of purple.

b   Paint the body of the butterfly using a light tone of brown.

c   Add shading and detail on the wings and body of the butterfly using neat purple.

6   Leave all the butterflies to dry while you paint the cake.

7   Paint the trail around the bottom tier of the cake using a medium tone of soft green. You may find it easier to use the size 0 brush as this will keep the trail thin and elegant. Don't paint in any leaves at this stage, as you will add these once you have painted the flowers.

8   **Method for painting the daisies** *(illustrated on page 136)*

a   Paint the petals of the daisies in white, using the size 4 brush. For some of the daisies you can paint all of the petals (to give the impression that you are viewing the flower from directly above), but others should be painted to give a side view by painting a semi-circle of petals (to leave room for the centre).

b   Using a medium tone of yellow add the centre of the daisies.

c   Once the petals have completely dried you can add some details. Create the effects of shadow at the inner edge of the petals (nearest to the centre) using a light tone of blue—you only need to add this shading to one side of the flower, and you should make sure you don't make the strokes too long. Colour the tips of the petals using a medium tone of pink, again making sure the strokes

2a 2b 2c

3a 3b 3c

4a 4b 4c

5a 5b 5c

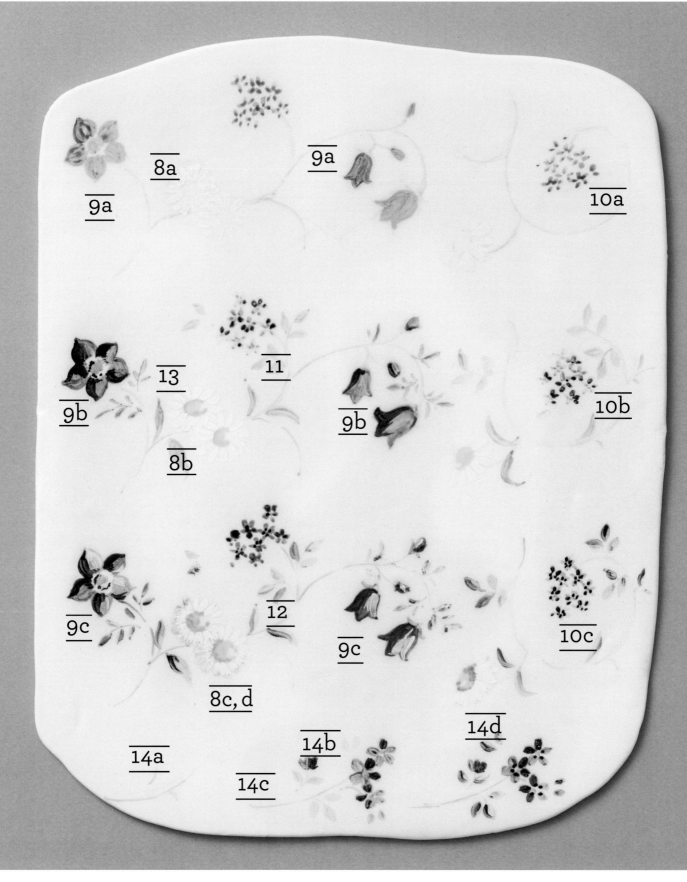

are very short (or the daisy will appear pink rather than being mostly white).

d   Shade the centre of the flowers with a medium tone of orange. Only shade one area of the centre, rather than all the way around.

9   Method for painting the bluebells

a   Using a light tone of purple, paint the first layer of colour with the size 4 brush. Some flowers will have five petals, as if viewing them directly from above, whereas others will have three petals, as if viewing them from the side.

b   Add neat purple to indicate shadow onto the side of the three-petalled flower and in the centre of the five-petalled flower.

c   Mix up some blue paint with a small amount of white to create a pastel blue colour. Paint this onto the bluebells to create the highlights.

10   Method for painting the forget-me-nots

a   Paint the petals of the flowers using a pale tone of blue. Each flower has five petals, but make sure to leave a clear space for the yellow centre: if you don't, you will find that the colours will merge and become muddy.

b   Paint over some of the pale blue petals with neat blue to indicate shadow. Leave the flowers to dry, then add a yellow centre.

c   Add small dots of dark brown at the end of each of the petals nearest the centre.

11   Use a light tone of soft green to paint in the forget-me-not and daisy leaves. The forget-me-not leaves are almond-shaped and are painted in sprigs of three. The daisy leaves are longer and thinner, and grow directly from the stalks.

12   Add shading on these leaves using neat soft green.

13   Paint the bluebell leaves using a medium tone of dark green. These leaves are in sprigs of four or five and are much thinner than the forget-me-not leaves.

14   Method for painting the top tier

a   Paint the stalks of the sprigs first using a medium tone of light green. If you are using the size 4 brush and find that your stalks are too thick, then switch to the size 0 brush.

b   Paint the flowers using the method described in Step 10 for the forget-me-nots, but paint half of the flowers using tones of purple with blue centres, and the other half with the blue tones and yellow centres. Using dark brown add dots to the inner points of the petals on all of the flowers.

c   Paint the leaves in sprigs of two or three using a light to medium tone of soft green.

d   Add shading to the leaves with neat dark green.

15   Method for finishing the cake

a   Glue the butterflies onto the cake with confectioners' glue (or you can use royal icing if you prefer). Hold each butterfly in place with your finger for a few seconds until it has stuck fast.

b   To attach the smallest butterfly to the top of the cake, roll a small piece of white fondant into a ball. Glue this to the top of the cake, where you wish to place the butterfly. Then glue the butterfly on top of the ball of fondant.

RUFFLED CUT-OUT CAKE

If you are nervous about attempting to paint a cake, then creating cut-out plaques is an easy way to help you get over that fear. With this method, you paint onto a sheet of fondant, cut out your design and then stick it onto the cake once it has dried. If you find that you're not happy with your painted cut-out, it is much less daunting to throw that away and make another one, rather than repaint a whole cake.

The following cake uses cut-out plaques, and is one of my most popular designs—who can resist a cake covered in romantic ruffles? But (and I'm letting you in on a closely guarded secret here) ruffles are incredibly easy to master, and imperfections will result in ruffles that have more character than immaculate ones. As a bonus, the layer of fondant below the ruffles is totally obscured, so a cake with poorly applied icing can be transformed into an elegant, beautiful design.

If you will be boxing this cake up, place it on an 11"/280 mm board, as the ruffles stand quite proud from the sides of the cake and you wouldn't want them to get crushed.

EQUIPMENT

Paintbrushes, sizes 8, 4, 0, and a brush for gluing

1 lb 9 oz/700 g modelling paste

Confectioners' glue

Tracing paper

Non-toxic pencil

Scalpel

Foam mat

Ruler or straight edge

Cocktail sticks

Mini rolling pin

Modelling ball tool

Colours

Pink, yellow, dark pink, orange, soft green, bright green, dark green, blue

A three-tiered cake consisting of 8"/200 mm, 6"/150 mm and 4"/100 mm square cakes, each covered in white fondant

<u>1</u> Method for painting the large plaque *(illustrated on page 141)*

a Roll out 3 ½ oz/100 g of modelling paste to a thickness of ¹⁄₁₆–⅛"/2–3 mm.

b Enlarge the template *(Template 24, page 226)* by 140%. Trace the design onto the fondant using the template.

c Mix up a medium tone of pink and use this to paint the rose, using the size 8 brush. Leave the areas where the petals would turn over on themselves unpainted, as this will indicate the light hitting the rose.

d Paint the largest of the five-petalled flowers using a light tone of blue.

e Paint in a number of the other smaller flowers with yellow. The flower next to the blue one should be left mostly white, but by adding a very few strokes of yellow and blue onto the petals you will indicate shadow.

f Paint the centres of the white and blue flowers in yellow, but leave an unpainted circle in the very middle (this will help to add more depth and interest to the flowers).

g Paint the two flowers which are viewed from side-on in a light tone of dark pink.

h Use light tones of both the soft green and bright green to paint the first layer of the leaves.

i Add shading to the rose with a darker tone of pink. Because this is more of a formal rose design (rather than the more impressionist roses we have painted in previous projects) each individual petal will require shading detail, but make sure that you paint most of the darker shading in the centre of the rose.

j Use a mid-tone of the blue to add details on the petals of the blue flower. Paint these marks so that they are moving from the edge of the petals into the centre. ⟶

k   Add details to the yellow flowers using the orange paint—this shading comes from the centre of the flowers and moves towards the edges of the petals.

l   Add some shading to the side-on flower with a medium tone of dark pink.

m   Paint details on the leaves using medium tones of soft green and dark green. Add green centres to the small yellow flowers, a small dot of green to the centre of the white flower, and a circle of pink to the centre of the blue flower.

n   Add the very darkest tone onto the rose with neat dark pink. Use this same colour to add another layer of shading onto the side-on flower.

o   Add a final layer of shading onto the blue flower with neat blue.

p   Paint another layer of detail onto the leaves using neat dark green.

q   Switch to the size 0 brush and use neat pink to paint an outline onto the flowers and leaves. Keep this a little loose—don't outline every single detail, and make some breaks in the line to add interest and give the design more movement. Add some small dots of the same colour around the centres of the yellow flowers.

r   Cut around the edge of the painting using a scalpel to create the plaque and leave it on a foam mat to harden. Usually a couple of hours will be enough for the plaque to harden and be strong enough to attach to the cake, but it is safer if you can leave it overnight. Ball together the leftover modelling paste.

2   Method for painting the small plaque

a   Roll out 1¾ oz/50 g of the modelling paste to a thickness of ¹⁄₁₆–⅛"/2–3 mm.

b   Enlarge the template (*Template 25, page 224*) by 145%. Trace the design onto the fondant using the template.

c   Mix up a light tone of pink and use it to paint the large flower with the size 8 brush. Paint the centre of the flower with yellow and use this colour for the small flower.

d   Paint some of the leaves with light tones of soft green and some with bright green. Paint the very centre of both of the flowers using the soft green tone.

e   Working from the edge of the petals into the centre of the flower, add details with a medium tone of pink. Add shadows to the ⟹

Drag the ball tool along the fondant

Paint glue along the top edge of the cake

yellow flower using the orange paint—you can also use this colour to add shading to the yellow centre of the pink flower.

f   Add shading onto the leaves and the very centres of the flowers with neat soft green. When that layer is dry, add a few darker touches with neat dark green.

g   Use neat pink to paint in a final few details on the tips of the pink petals and the centre of the yellow flower.

h   Switch to the size 0 brush and add a neat dark pink outline around the whole design using the same method described in step 1q for the large plaque.

i   Cut out the plaque using the scalpel and leave it to dry on a foam mat.

3   Method for creating the ruffles

a   Roll out a 1¾ oz/50 g ball of the modelling paste to a thickness of ¹⁄₃₂"/1 mm.

b   Cut out a strip measuring ¾ x 10"/20 x 250 mm. Don't be tempted to make longer strips than this, as they would be untenable to work with. The strip doesn't need to be perfect and have totally straight lines—any unevenness will just add to the wave effect of the ruffles. Ball up the excess fondant and place it in some plastic wrap to make sure that it doesn't dry out while you're ruffling the strip.

c   Place the strip onto a foam mat. Starting at one end of the strip, place your ball tool halfway down the strip, and push down onto the fondant. As you are pressing down, gently drag the ball tool off the top of the fondant strip. This will thin the edge of the strip and create a lovely wavy movement. Keep applying the ball tool in this fashion along the length of the strip. If you find that the edge of the strip is breaking, then the fondant is too dry. Knead a small amount of boiled water into the modelling paste and roll out your strip again—the ruffles should be much smoother.

d   Paint a strip of glue around the top edge of the bottom tier cake. Apply the ruffled strip to the glue, making sure to only stick the bottom (unruffled) part of the strip. The remaining part of the

Apply the ruffled strip

Glue the last ruffle and bend it back

strip should be loose. Watch that the strip doesn't fall back on itself, and gently guide the ruffles into the position you require to give it a wavy effect—some ruffles can bend out from the cake and some can bend inwards.

e   Continue to make more strips with the modelling paste and glue them around the cake. When you have completed the first ruffle, start the next one about ½"/10 mm below it; the second layer of ruffles should cover the bottom edge of the ruffle above. Carry on in this fashion, adding more layers—I normally find that seven rows of ruffles will cover this cake. Try to make sure that you don't align any joins in the ruffles above each other, and continue to create waves in the ruffles.

f   When there is a ½"/10 mm gap left at the bottom of the cake, make the final row of ruffles. Begin these strips in the same manner as described above, but once you have ruffled the strip, then cut it in half lengthways—use a ruler or a straight edge for this, as this is the edge that you will see on the cake. Glue it to the very bottom edge of the cake and then bend back the ruffle to try and cover as much of the cut edge as you can—it's fine if it bends over and touches the cake board in places, this will add to the effect.

4   Glue the large plaque onto the right hand side of the middle tier. You may need to hold it in place for a minute or so until it has stuck firmly.

5   Glue the small plaque to the left hand side of the top tier. Again, keep holding it until you can feel it is stuck firmly to the cake.

ROSETTE CAKE

Give this cake first prize! In fact, it seems to have picked up bronze, silver, *and* gold. I can only imagine that it has won a prettiness competition! It would be easy for you to change the flowers on this design to roses, hydrangeas, or even bluebells.

EQUIPMENT

Paintbrushes, sizes 8, 4, 0, and a brush for gluing

7 oz/200 g modelling paste

Confectioners' glue

Non-toxic pencil

Scalpel

Foam mat

3 circle cutters, sizes 2½"/65 mm, 2"/50 mm, 1¾"/45 mm

Modelling ball tool

Double-sided sticky tape

Colours

Pink, yellow, purple, soft green, dark green, blue

A three-tiered cake consisting of 10"/250 mm, 8"/200 mm, and 6"/150 mm cakes, each covered in white fondant

3 lengths of ribbon, 21½"/540 mm, 27½"/698 mm, 33½"/850 mm long

1 **Method for creating the rosettes** (*illustrated on page 146-7*)

a   Roll out 1¾ oz/50 g of the modelling paste to a thickness of ⅛ – 3/16"/ 3-4 mm. Cut out three discs from the fondant using each of the different-sized cutters, then leave them to firm up on a foam mat.

b   Colour 1¾ oz/50 g of the modelling paste dark pink. Roll out the dark pink modelling paste until it is no more than 1/32"/1 mm thick. Cut out a strip of the paste measuring roughly 1¼ x 17"/30 x 430 mm. You don't need to make it perfectly straight, as any wobbly edges will add to the ruffled finish.

c   Place the strip on a foam mat. Starting at one end, place the ball tool in the middle of the strip (widthways) and push down onto the fondant. As you are pressing down, move the ball tool off the edge of the strip. This will thin the edge of the strip and create a lovely wavy movement. Keep moving the ball tool in this fashion along the length of the strip. If you find that the edge of the strip is breaking, then your fondant is too dry. Knead a small amount of boiled water into the modelling paste and roll out the strip again—the ruffles should be much smoother now.

d   Paint a ¼"/5 mm strip of confectioners' glue on the edge of the largest circle.

e   Stick the unruffled edge of the fondant strip to the glue on the fondant circle, making folds in the strip every ½-¾"/10-20 mm. As you stick the last piece of the strip down, fold the edge under to keep it neat. Repeat the same process as above for the other dark pink rosettes. Because the rosettes decrease in size you will need to cut out smaller strips—use a strip measuring 1 x 12"/25 x 300 mm for the 2"/50 mm circle, and ⅝ x 8"/ 15 x 200 mm for the 1¾"/45 mm circle. Only roll out and ruffle one strip at a time, as if you roll out the fondant and then leave it too long before you use the ball tool, you will find that the edge of the strip will crack and break.

f   Take a 4"/100 mm width of plastic wrap, squash it together to create a sausage shape and then form it into a circle. Place this under the edges of the ruffles while they firm. This will prevent the ruffles from drooping (no one wants a droopy ruffle!).

g   Colour 1¼"/35 g of the modelling paste light pink.

→

Cut out discs, *step 1a*

Move the ball tool over the fondant, *step 1c*

Paint glue around the largest disc, *step 1d* ⟹

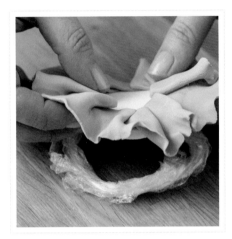

Place the rosette on plastic wrap, *step 1f*

Leave to harden, *step 1f*

Drag the ball tool over the fondant, *step 1j* ⟹

Make folds, *step 1k*

Place the painted disc in the middle, *step 1o*

Press down gently, *step 1o* ⟹

Place the strip onto the disc, *step 1e*

Make folds, *step 1e*

Fold the edge under, *step 1e*

Ruffle the whole strip, *step 1j*

Glue the inner edge of the first ruffle, *step 1k*

Place the light pink strip on the disc, *step 1k*

Leave to harden, *step 1o*

h   Roll out the light pink fondant until it is no more than ¹⁄₃₂"/1 mm thick.

i   Cut out a strip measuring 1¼ x 10"/35 x 250 cm.

j   Create ruffles with the ball tool using the same method as above.

k   Glue the inner edge of the dark pink ruffle on the largest circle. Place the light pink strip on the glue using the method described above. Leave the ruffled circle to become firm again using the sausage of plastic wrap to prop it up. To create the light pink ruffles for the other two rosettes you need a strip measuring ¾ x 10"/20 x 250 mm for the second rosette and a strip measuring ½ x 6"/10 x 150 mm for the small rosette. Then follow the steps above (h–k).

2   Place the lengths of ribbon around the bottom of each cake tier. Secure the ends of the ribbons with small pieces of double-sided sticky tape.

3   Roll out the remaining white modelling paste to a thickness of ¹⁄₃₂"/1 mm or less, and cut out circles measuring 2"/50 mm, 1¾"/45 mm and 1¼"/30 mm. Leave the discs to dry slightly.

4   Draw the outline of a pansy onto the largest disc with a pencil or a size 0 paintbrush with a very light tone of brown.

5   Mix up a light tone of purple and use the size 4 brush to paint the top two petals of the pansy. Start the brushstroke at the outside edge of the petal and move towards the middle of the flower. As you reach the end of the stroke, reduce pressure on the brush and lift the bristles off the fondant—this creates a soft mark which recreates the flower's markings. Paint the other three petals of the pansy in the same fashion but make the marks shorter, so that you are painting only a third of the petal.

6   With the size 4 brush, paint the yellow centre of the flower. This time, start the stroke near the centre of the flower (leave a circle of unpainted white fondant in the very centre) and lift the brush off the fondant after you have painted roughly a third of the petal with the colour.

7   Use a mid-tone of the purple and add some detail onto the outer edges of the petals. Once again, paint from the edge of the petal into the centre.

8   When you are sure that the yellow colour has dried completely (or you will end up with a nasty brown pansy) paint neat purple in the centre of the flower, painting from the centre of the flower to the outside edge of the petals. Make the strokes slightly longer in the middle of the bottom petal.

9   Paint a green centre in the very middle of the flower.

10   Take a small ball of fondant and stick it to the centre of the largest rosette using confectioners' glue. Making sure you don't smudge any paint, glue the back of the disc and stick it onto the ball of fondant. You will find this easier if the disc is still pliable, as it will bend slightly and stick to the rosette more firmly.

11   Paint the other two discs with pansies using the method described above. You can change the main colours of the pansies if you wish, but always use the neat purple for the centre detailing.

12   Glue the rosettes to the cake. You can place them in a vertical line in the middle of the tiers, but I prefer a diagonal line.

13   **Method for painting the cake**

a   The flowers are painted just on the sides of each cake. They are fairly spaced apart and do not interact with each other. Make sure not to create a repeating pattern of flowers or colours around the sides of the cakes. Because these flowers are very small and have fairly basic shapes, I would advise you to paint them freehand—using an outline will create stiffer flowers

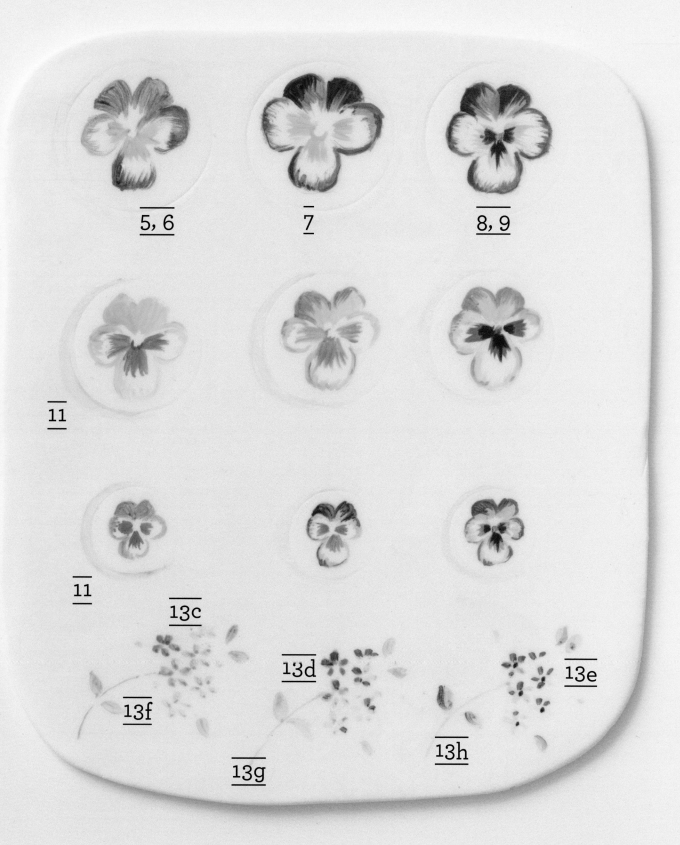

<u>5, 6</u>

<u>7</u>

<u>8, 9</u>

<u>11</u>

<u>11</u>

<u>13c</u>

<u>13d</u>

<u>13e</u>

<u>13f</u>

<u>13g</u>

<u>13h</u>

and possibly make the colours feel muddy.

b   Paint the heads of the pansy flowers using the method
    described above for the pansies on the rosettes.

c   Using a light tone of the blue, paint the first layer
    of the spray of blue flowers. Each flower is made up
    of five small petals. The flowers should be closely
    grouped together so that there is not much white
    space in between them.

d   Paint over some of the flower petals with a mid-tone
    of the blue.

e   Add a dot of neat blue to the centre of each
    individual flower.

f   You can use the size 4 brush to paint the stalks,
    but if they look too thick switch to the size 0 brush.
    A pansy stalk grows from the side of the flower
    rather than directly from below the bottom petal.
    Give each stalk a slight bend.

g   Paint the leaves using a mid-tone of the green paint;
    the leaves of the pansies should be slightly plump,
    and only add two to three per stalk. The leaves for
    the blue flowers are smaller and thinner, you can
    add more per stalk, from five to seven.

h   Add detail on the leaves using neat dark green paint.

GOLD CAKE

Many times during my working life as a designer and artist I've turned to gold paint to jazz up a design; even in my teens I always had a pot of gold ink ready to flick over any and every work of art I produced. So you can imagine my delight when I came across edible gold paint in a spray can! Fortunately this happened just before the birthday of a close friend. She was going to be blowing out candles on a gold cake that year.

When using gold spray, you need to create a spray booth to prevent your house turning gold. This can be a cardboard box that comfortably fits the cake. Cut the top flaps off the box and stand it on its side (so what was the top of the box is now the side facing you), and you have created a spray booth. If the weather permits, I suggest doing any spraying outdoors. When spraying, wear a mask to protect your lungs.

I have classified this as an advanced project for a couple of reasons.

The first is that there are three layers of painting. The initial layer acts as a rough guide for the design, the second layer is the gold paint. Before you can paint the final layer, you need to wash off any gold paint sitting on top of the flowers and leaves.

You have to be confident in your painting skills to cope with all these layers. You need to paint the design freehand. If you trace the design, you will soon lose any guidelines because of all the layers.

I recommend that if you don't have any previous painting experience, you try some of the less difficult projects first. If you are determined to "get your gold on," attempt a cookie or cupcake version first.

EQUIPMENT

Paintbrushes, sizes 8, 4, 0

2 x 100 ml cans of edible gold spray

Colours

Pink, yellow, dark pink, orange, purple, soft green, bright green, dark green, blue, white, brown

A three-tiered cake consisting of 10"/250 mm, 8"/200 mm, and 6"/150 mm cakes, covered in ochre-coloured fondant (you make ochre by kneading in yellow and brown edible colours)

Cut roses for decoration (optional)

1 Method for the first layer

a This layer is created by painting the rough shapes of the elements onto the cake. Don't spend too much time on this because it is just to provide an indication of where you will place the flowers after the cake has been sprayed with the gold paint. If you wish, you can sketch the outline of the flowers so that you know that they will be evenly spaced around the cake.

b You should be able to fit three bunches (although I use that term loosely as they are quite freeform bunches) around the cake. I have given you the detailed instructions for two bunches. The third bunch you can create by mixing elements of the other two groups together to fill the space.

c Mix up a medium to dark tone of the dark pink paint and use this and your size 8 brush to paint the two large flowers in the first bunch. Use the same colour to paint some buds in groups of three or five.

d Use a medium tone of soft green to paint the large leaves around the two flowers you have painted and the stalks for the buds.

e Mix up a medium tone of purple and use this to paint the five-petal flowers and the buds that are floating away from the bunch. Then use the a medium tone of soft green to paint some leaves next to these purple flowers.

f Paint the second bunch of flowers in a similar manner, but use pink for one of the five-petal flowers and all the buds. $\Longrightarrow$

g The third bunch needs to be large enough to fill the remaining space on the cake. Make up your own group of flowers using a mixture of the different elements from the first two bunches. Consider the flowers' colours in relation to the flowers surrounding them. You can add interest by painting two flowers of the same colour next to each other, but three of the same together creates a strong line of colour which overwhelms the rest of the design.

h You will also need to add a few elements on the base of the bottom tier to fill in any gaps. If you have gaps further up the cake, paint a floating five-petalled flower or a spray of buds.

2 After about 15 minutes the first layer of paint should be dry enough for you to add the gold. Place your cake in the spray box and spray the first layer of gold onto the cake according to the instructions on the can. Leave it to dry.

3 Spray a second layer of gold onto the cake and leave it to dry. If you feel that the gold is still looking a bit thin and not lustrous enough you can spray a third layer onto the cake. You should still be able to see an impression of the flowers and leaves under the layer of gold, but don't worry if some of the smaller elements have disappeared.

4 Use a size 8 brush loaded with clean water to wash off the gold sitting on top of the painted flowers and leaves (if you paint straight onto the gold the colour will turn really muddy). Wet the area and then pull off the water with the paintbrush and a sheet of paper towels. You will probably need to repeat this process two or three times to get all the gold off. Most of the first layer of paint will also be removed at this point. Watch out for any runs of water down the side of the cake or any drips on the tops of the tiers because it will be hard to correct any mistakes. You will find that you need to change your water two or three times in this process as it will quickly become saturated with gold

particles. Don't worry if the water bleeds a little into the gold paint around the flowers and leaves—this all adds to the texture of the design.

5 Leave the fondant to dry.

6 Method for painting the first group of flowers
a Mix up a light tone of pink and use this to paint the centre of the rose, adding a few marks of this colour onto the body of the rose.
b Use a medium tone of dark pink to paint the outer petals of the chrysanthemum. Start your brushstroke at the outer edge of a petal and move it towards the centre, gradually releasing pressure on the brush as you do so.
c Mix up a light tone of the purple and use this to paint the five-petalled flowers and the buds around them.
d Use a medium tone of dark pink to paint the remaining buds on this grouping.
e Mix up a medium tone of soft green and paint the leaves—remember to paint in the direction of the veins and to leave some areas unpainted. Using the same tone, paint any stalks for the buds, switching to the size 4 brush to achieve lovely thin lines.
f Mix up some white paint and use this to paint the inner petals of the chrysanthemum. You need to try and pick up some of the pink colour below this layer and incorporate it into the white. But take extra care not to create flat, toneless petals. You can use two colours on your brush at the same time to get around this problem—one side of the brush has white paint and the other side dark pink paint. As you paint the petals, the colours will merge together, creating an interesting mark. Leave the centre of the flower unpainted.
g Add white paint to the dark pink buds. Give some of the buds more white than others to create a more attractive design.
h Using the two-colours-on-a-brush technique, paint the purple flowers and buds with a mixture of white and purple. Leave the centres of these flowers unpainted.

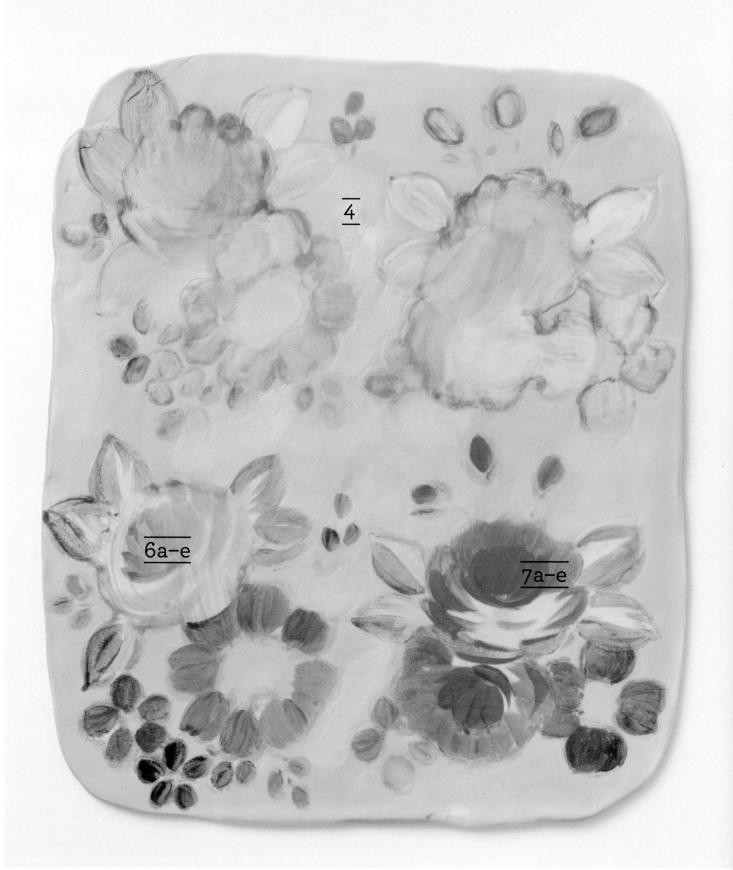

i Add more white brush marks to the rose, painting these marks in the direction of the petals.

j Paint white highlights onto the leaves. Work into some of these marks to give the white paint a slight green tint.

k Mix up a medium tone of pink and use this to paint the centre petals of the rose.

l Add some neat purple to the inner point of the petals of the purple flowers and buds. Paint neat dark pink onto one side of the centre of these flowers.

m Paint neat dark pink marks onto the centre of the chrysanthemum. Then add neat pink to the centre of the rose, mirroring the petals that you have already painted.

n Add shading to the leaves using soft green, then once this colour has dried, add a few strokes using dark green.

o Add a small amount of neat dark pink in the very centre of the rose.

7 Method for painting the second group of flowers

a Paint the first rose using a medium tone of pink. Leave an area under the centre of the rose unpainted—this will indicate the lightest area of the rose. Keep your brush marks loose and flowing. Paint the rose buds this colour, and the smaller five-petalled flower.

b Mix up a medium tone of the dark pink and paint this onto the second rose, again leaving some areas unpainted.

c Paint the large five-petalled flower with a medium tone of purple. Start your brush mark at the outer edge of the petal and bring it in towards the centre of the flower, releasing pressure on the brush as it moves.

d Mix up a dark tone of pink and paint the centre of the first rose, then add this colour to the side of the rose, leaving some of the first layer unpainted.

Repeat this process using the dark pink colour on the second rose.

e Paint a dark soft green tone onto the leaves, making sure that your brush marks mirror the direction of the veins.

f Paint white highlights onto all the elements of the group, using the same technique employed for the first group. You may find that the centre of the roses need to be redefined after using the white paint.

g Paint neat soft green onto the leaves and a few dots on one side of the centre of the purple flower.

h Paint neat pink in the centre of the first rose and add a few marks in this colour to the side of the flower. Repeat this process using neat dark pink for the second flower.

i Use neat purple to add some shading onto the petals of the purple flower—just paint this on the inside tip of the petals. Repeat this process using neat pink on the smaller pink flower.

j Add some neat dark green strokes to the leaves and the centre of the purple flower. You can also add a few thin strokes of neat pink onto the edge of some of the leaves.

k Using neat dark pink, paint final shading for the centre of the pink rose. Use neat purple to do the same in the centre of the dark pink rose.

8 Paint the remaining flowers using the techniques described for the first two groups.

9 If you have any marks and imperfections left on the fondant, spray a small amount of the gold onto your palette. Paint it very carefully with the size 8 brush onto the marks. This technique will only work for very small areas. If you have larger mistakes, paint a leaf or small flower over it.

10 If you wish, decorate the completed cake with cut roses, but make sure they are completely dry.

CUPCAKE PROJECTS

Despite all the predictions of the doomsayers, the trend for cupcakes shows absolutely no signs of slowing down. I think this is because, while a slice of gooey cake is always delicious, serve that same cake up into cupcake wrappers, and it immediately becomes something more delicate and exquisite. These precious individual portions make the receiver of the confection feel that much more special. And, speaking as a baker, I find it much easier (and infinitely quicker) to whip up a batch of cupcakes rather than wrestle with a large cake, which is why cupcakes are my go-to goodies when called upon to provide a batch of something tasty for my children's class cake sales.

There are still many couples who prefer cupcake towers instead of a wedding cake, and adding a cellophane-wrapped cupcake into a party bag is much more preferable than a serviette-encrusted slice of sticky, stale cake.

I have created some beautiful painted cupcake projects for you that would be just perfect for any event you can imagine (excluding a zombie apocalypse!) and, to make this even better, they are all fairly easy to accomplish with aplomb—even for a beginner.

BUTTERFLY CUPCAKES

I love sitting outside on a summer's evening with a glass of something cold and fizzy, feeling the warmth of the lingering evening sun on my face and watching the insects and butterflies flit about. Obviously (because I live in the UK) this is a very rare occurrence: our usual summer weather is rainy, cloudy, and sometimes, for a change, comes with gale force winds! So on these occasions I like to cheer myself up with a delicious summery cupcake, and butterflies are such an absolute signifier of summer that they are the obvious choice to use for a topper.

The butterflies in this project are painted with the simplest design, making them a perfect project for beginners, or even children.

The butterflies can be made well in advance and can be stored in a cardboard box until you need them.

If you are making this project for a cupcake tower, my advice would be to place all the cupcakes on to the cake stand first and add the butterflies at the last possible minute. This will prevent the fondant butterflies from wilting.

You can easily change the colours used to match a specific colour palette. If you want dark-coloured butterflies, then use a white paint for the flowers, but just be aware that there may be strange colours mixed into the base tone that can bleed through the white, so always experiment with your colours first to prevent any nasty shocks.

EQUIPMENT

Paintbrush, size 4

3½ oz/100 g white modelling paste

Small butterfly cutter

Cardboard cut into strips and folded lengthways along the middle

Edible glitter (optional)

Colours

Yellow

12 cupcakes decorated with yellow buttercream swirls

1. Roll out the modelling paste until it is $1/32$–$1/16$"/1–2 mm thick.

2. Cut out 14 butterflies (I always make a few extra in case of breakages). Very gently fold the butterflies in half and lay them on top of the cardboard (see page 134). Leave them until they are dry (at least overnight).

3. Use the size 4 brush to paint the simple yellow flowers on top of the butterflies. Leave them to dry overnight.

4. Place each butterfly gently on top of a cupcake. You can add edible glitter to the cakes at this point, if you like.

SIMPLE ROSE TOPPERS ●●

These cupcakes are sweet and pretty—and how can you ever go wrong with a rose? I have created two designs: a single rose and a wreath of rosebuds. They have been created to match the Single Rose Cake (page 106). Together, with the cake, you can create a romantic cupcake tower and cutting cake which would be perfect for a wedding or a very special afternoon tea.

EQUIPMENT

Paintbrushes, size 4, 0

3½ oz/100 g modelling paste

Circle cutter measuring about 5.5 cm

Small rolling pin

Foam mat

Colours

Pink, dark pink, white, soft green, dark green, brown

12 cupcakes decorated with pale pink buttercream swirls

1. Colour the modelling paste a light tone of dark pink. Roll it out to a thickness of $1/16$"/2 mm and cut out 14 circles (always make a few extra in case of breakages). Leave the discs to dry on the foam until they are firm.

2. Reduce the template for the Single Rose Cake (*Template 3, page 224*) by 50% and transfer the designs onto the prepared discs using tracing paper (of course, you can paint these designs freehand if you wish).

3. Mix up a very pale pink tone and, with your size 4 brush, create the petals of the single rose, making sure that you paint the rose right in the centre of the disc. Paint the rosebuds on a disc for the second design, leaving enough space for the leaves. Add the stalks of the wreath. If you find your stalks are not fine enough then switch to the size 0 brush. Paint in the first layer of the leaves using pale soft green.

4. Mix up a slightly darker pink tone and work into the centre of the single rose. Add some of the darker pink to one side of the rose to create the effect of shadow. You can add a little of the darker pink to the rosebuds.

5. Paint neat soft green onto the leaves, remembering to paint in the direction of the leaf veins.

6. Add a few strokes of white on to the lighter side of the single rose, but take care not to go overboard with this colour, or you will deaden the flower. You can also paint a few highlights of the white onto the leaves. As well as adding a little white to the leaves of the wreath design, you can place a small dot of white at the top of each bud.

7. Use neat dusky pink to paint the centre of the rose and add a few strokes of this colour to one side of the flower. Do not merge these marks or you will pull the centre of the flower down. Paint a very small amount of dusky pink on the rosebuds to indicate shadow.

8. Use neat dark green to add lowlights to the leaves of the single rose.

3

4, 5

6-8

EASTER DUCKLING CUPCAKES

These are adorable little cupcakes, ideal for an Easter treat, and you can always add some chocolate chunks to the cupcake mix, which would make them appropriate for the season. If you were so inclined, you could even paint names onto the cupcakes to create name places for Easter lunch (see the Named Cookie project for more details about the method, page 203). The ducklings are outlined in brown, but not with one thick line—you use a series of small dashes to create a charming fluffy effect. This technique can also be used for teddy bears, fluffy hair, pom-poms, or really anything that needs a fuzzy or furry appearance.

EQUIPMENT

Paintbrushes, sizes 4, 0

Tracing paper

Non-toxic pencil

Colours

Pink, orange, yellow, blue, soft green, brown

12 cupcakes covered in white fondant domes

1. Using the template *(Template 27, page 225)*, trace the outline of the duckling onto the middle of the fondant dome using the template . If you find this too tricky (because of the shape of the dome), then either draw the outline freehand or cut out the template and draw around that.

2. Paint the body of the duckling with a medium tone of yellow, using the size 4 brush.

3. Add neat yellow to the back of the duckling and the bottom of the wing. Paint neat orange onto the beak and feet.

4. Use a medium tone of soft green to paint the grass around the duckling's feet. To create a lovely grass effect, start the mark at the bottom of the stalk of grass, then flick your paintbrush up—this will make the tip of the stalk thinner and lighter than the base.

5. At this stage, you can add bows to the ducklings, a pink one on the top of the head for a girl and a blue one under the beak for a boy.

6. Switch to the size 0 brush and paint the outline of the duckling with neat brown. To create the fluffy effect of the feathers don't paint in one line, use small marks around the edge. You can add a few marks on the body of the duckling, which will emphasise its fluffiness. Paint some detail on the grass.

7. Finish the cupcakes with a row of yellow dots around the edge of the fondant.

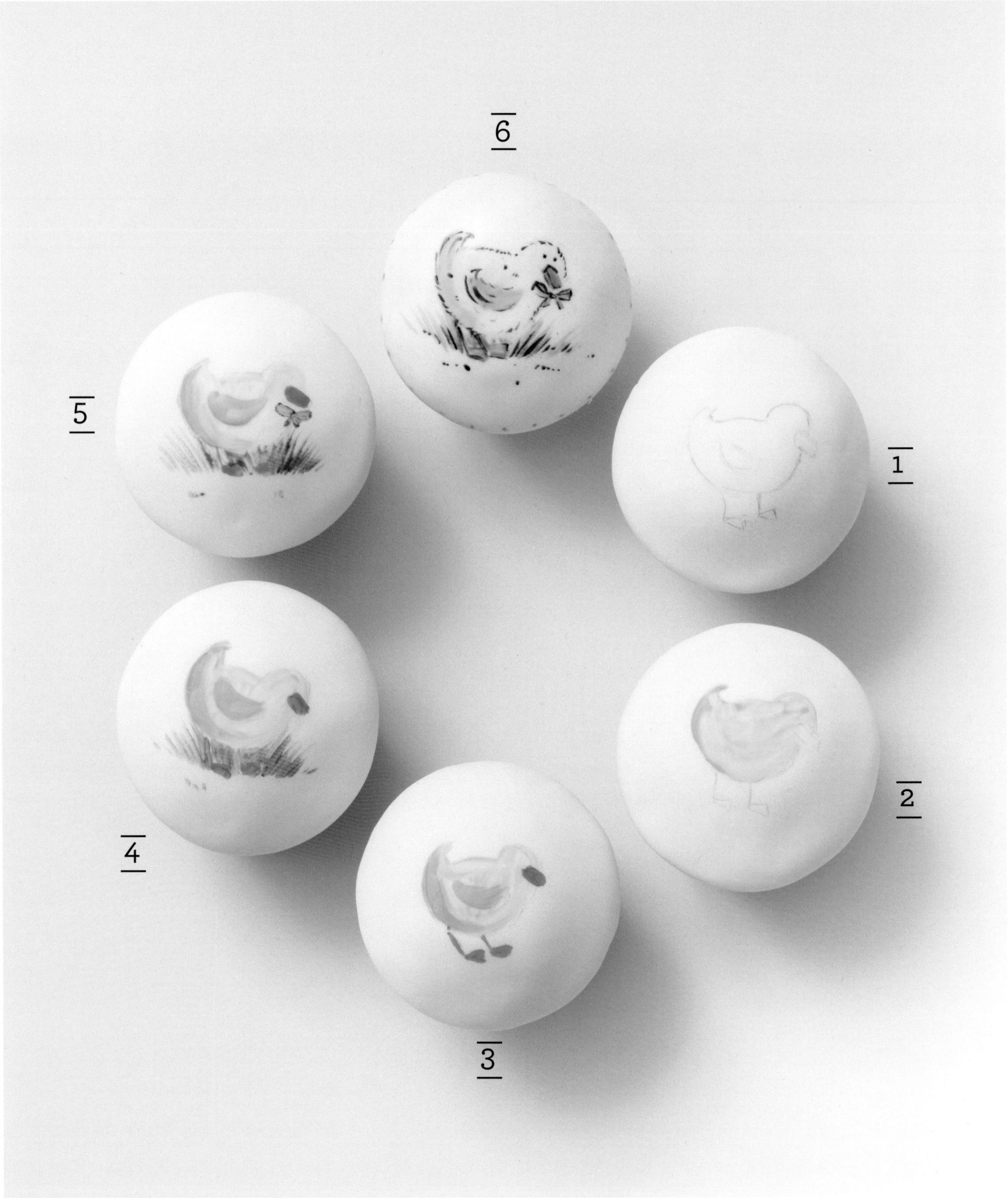
1
2
3
4
5
6

TATTOO CUPCAKES

Tattoo cakes have become quite fashionable for couples who are looking for quirky individual wedding cakes. It would be a "piece of cake" to create a striking cupcake tower using these tattoo hearts as toppers for such a joyous event.

You could make a single cake to give to your own special Valentine. The wording on the topper can be changed to make it relevant to any celebration or event. Do an online search for "free tattoo font" and you should be able to find a choice of fonts that you can download for non-commercial use at no cost. Print out your message using your font (in the size required) and trace it onto the banner first, or dive right in and paint it freehand. Don't be too concerned if the letters aren't painted perfectly—it is a tattoo design, and shouldn't look as if you have printed the letters on.

EQUIPMENT

Paintbrushes, sizes 8, 4, 0, and a brush for gluing

3½ oz/100 g white modelling paste

Confectioners' glue

Scalpel

Foam mat (optional)

Heart cutter, about 2½"/60 mm high x 2"/50 mm wide

Cocktail sticks

Colours

Black, red, blue

12 cupcakes decorated with red buttercream swirls

1. Colour 2¾ oz/80 g of the modelling paste red. Roll it out to a depth of roughly ¹/₁₆"/2 mm. Cut out 14 hearts (two are extras in case of breakages).

2. Roll out the remaining ¾ oz/20 g of white modelling paste to ¹/₁₆"/2 mm thickness. Use a scalpel to cut around the template provided for the banners (*Template 26, page 225*).

3. With the size 8 brush and neat red, on one side of the heart paint a line of shadow. Paint the black outline with the size 0 brush. Leave a small gap between the edge of the heart and the black line.

4. Using the size 4 brush and the blue paint, add in the shadows on the banner.

5. When the blue shadow is dry, you can trace the lettering onto the banners, or you can paint the letters freehand. Then paint the outline of the banner.

6. Leave the elements of the toppers to dry overnight, preferably on a foam mat. Then glue the banners onto the hearts.

7. Roll out the remaining red modelling paste to ¹/₁₆"/2 mm thickness. Cut out 14 rectangles that measure ⅝ x 1¼"/15 x 30 mm. Paint one side of the rectangle with glue. Do not use too much glue, as it will take longer to dry.

8. Turn the tattoo hearts over and place a cocktail stick on the back of each one. Then place a rectangle over the stick and gently press down so that it holds the cocktail stick firmly in position. Leave the hearts upside down until the glue is dry; store in a non-airtight box until the cupcakes are ready.

9. To serve, gently put a heart in the centre of each cupcake swirl.

TROPICAL CUPCAKES ● ● ●

I love the bright cheeriness of tropical flowers. They have a solidity that more traditional romantic garden flowers sometimes lack. Even though I live in a fairly cold, wet climate, I like imagining eating these cupcakes while lazing by a pool and drinking a cocktail . . . happy days!

EQUIPMENT

Paintbrushes, sizes 4, 0, and a brush for gluing

3½ oz/100 g white modelling paste

Confectioners' glue

Foam mat

Circle cutter, about 2"/50 mm

Cocktail sticks

Colours

Pink, orange, yellow, white, purple, bright green

12 cupcakes decorated with lime green buttercream swirls

1 Divide the modelling paste into three portions, and colour one portion pastel pink, one pastel orange and the last yellow.

2 Roll out each colour to a thickness of $^{1}/_{32}$–$^{1}/_{16}$"/1–2 mm, then cut out four circles from each colour (cut out a few extra circles in case of breakages). Leave the discs on a foam mat to firm up overnight.

3 With the size 8 brush, run a strip of colour around the edge of each disc—for the yellow disc use yellow paint, pink paint for the pink disc and orange for the orange disc. Make sure to blend it in so that you aren't left with a hard edge of colour. Leave the discs to dry before you paint the flowers onto them.

4 **Method for painting the pink discs** (*illustrated on page 177*)

a Mix together white and yellow. Using the size 4 brush, paint the outline of the petals, then paint strokes of colour, starting at the outline and moving towards the centre of the flowers. You are, in effect, creating a thick outline with a broken edge—I call this technique feathering.

b Fill in the rest of the flower with orange paint, again trying to keep the edge where it meets the yellow paint feathered.

c Paint pink in the centre of the flower, mirroring the orange paint.

d Mix together bright green and white paint and, in the very centre of the flower, paint the tiny stalks of the stamens. Paint the bean-shaped top of the stamen using neat pink (these elements should be neat and refined, so you can always switch to a size 0 brush if they seem too thick).

e With either a size 4 or size 0 brush, paint neat purple dots around the centre of the flower and add a thin line (in the shape of a smile) to indicate the very centre of the flower.

5 **Method for painting the orange discs** (*illustrated on page 177*)

a Paint the outline of the flower using a medium tone of pink, and then brush feathery marks from the outline towards the centre of the flower, covering about a third of the petal.

b Brush orange paint from the edge of the pink shading towards the flower's centre, keeping the brush light on the fondant to create feathery marks. ⟹

Lay a cocktail stick on the back of the disc

Glue a rectangle of fondant over the stick

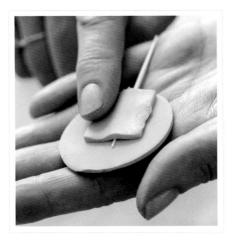

Press down firmly to adhere

c   Brush white paint from the centre of the flower to the edge of the orange paint. Use neat orange to create the centre line of the flower.
d   Paint the stamens using bright green for the stalks and neat red for the tips. Add neat red detailing on the edge of the petals.
e   Using purple, add shading to the stamens and some small dots around the centre.

6   **Method for painting the yellow discs** (*see opposite*)
a   Mix together white and pink paint and draw the outline of the petals. Fill in the centre of the flower with the pale pink, leaving the area for the stamen unpainted. Add some feathery brush marks in this colour, moving your paintbrush from the centre of the flower to the edge of the petals.
b   Add darker feathery marks to the edge of the petals using a medium tone of pink.
c   Paint the stamen of the flower initially with a mix of the bright green and white and then add some shading with neat bright green.
d   Using neat pink, paint in some darker marks on the tips of the petals, then add a small amount of shading to the centre of the flower.
e   Paint a few thin white lines over the pale pink using the size 0 brush.

7   Once all the discs are dry, turn them onto their backs. Roll out the remaining coloured fondants and cut out small rectangles roughly 1¼ x ½"/30 x 10 mm, and paint these with confectioners' glue. Lay a cocktail stick on the back of each painted disc, roughly two-thirds of the way up. Stick the rectangle of fondant over the cocktail stick, pressing down firmly to adhere, and leave it to dry before sitting each disc in a cupcake.

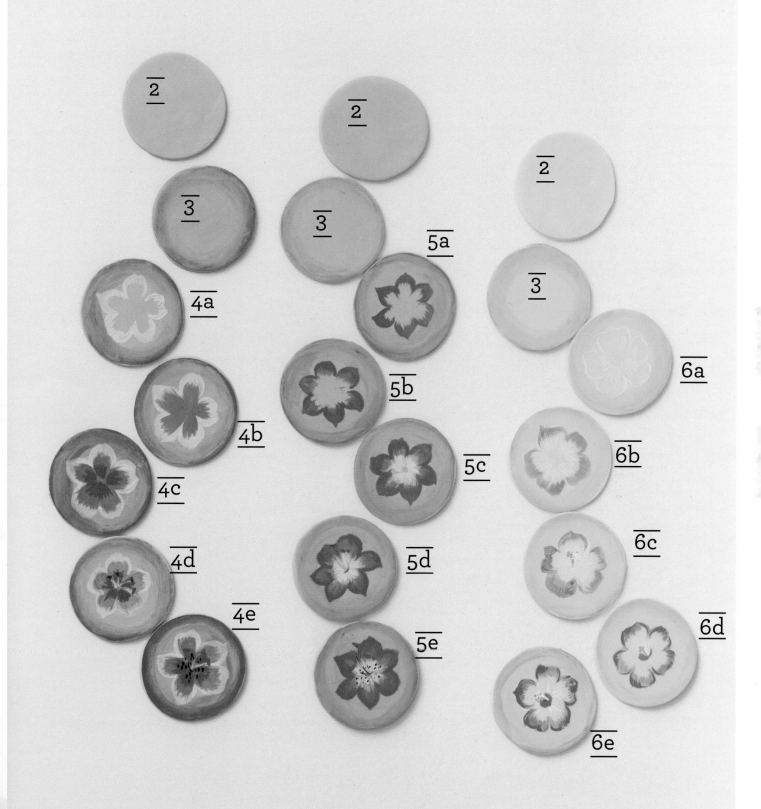

TEACUP CUPCAKES ● ● ●

Many cake decorators present their cupcakes in a teacup, a style I admire. I decided to take it one step further and create a project which adds a mini teacup to the top of the cupcake in the teacup! Don't forget to keep a crook in your pinky finger when eating these confections.

EQUIPMENT

Paintbrushes, sizes 4, 0, and a brush for gluing

5½ oz/150 g modelling paste

Confectioners' glue

Scalpel

Circle cutters, 1½"/40 mm and ¾"/20 mm

Cocktail sticks

Plastic wrap

Colours

Pink, orange, yellow, blue, soft green, dark green, gold

12 cupcakes covered in white fondant domes

<u>1</u> Method for creating the teacups and saucers

a Colour a quarter of the modelling paste pale pink, a quarter pale blue and a quarter pale yellow, and leave the remaining paste white.

b Roll out the paste to a depth of ¹⁄₃₂–¹⁄₁₆"/1-2 mm.

c Cut out the saucer using the larger cutter, then take the small cutter and gently press it in to the middle of the saucer shape. Make four of each colour (I always make a few extra in case of any breakages).

d Roll a small piece of plastic wrap into a sausage. Wrap the ends together to create a 1¼"/30 mm circle. Place the saucer on top of the plastic wrap. Gently push down the middle of the paste to form a saucer shape.

e Cut out the teacup shapes using the template (*Templates 28-31, page 227*), cutting out four of each colour (again, making a few extras).

<u>2</u> Method for making the white teacup and saucer

a Use a pale to medium tone of blue and, with the size 4 brush, paint shading onto the teacup and saucer.

b Use a light tone of pink to paint the rose and rosebuds on the teacup and saucer. Paint in the leaves with a medium tone of soft green. Use the size 0 brush to paint the stalks of the rosebuds on the saucer.

c Switch back to the size 4 brush and paint the centre of the rose with neat pink and add some small details onto the rosebuds with the same colour. Add shading to the leaves with dark green.

d Paint gold edges on the teacup and the saucer.

<u>3</u> Method for painting the pink teacup and saucer

a Use a pale to medium tone of blue and the size 4 brush to paint shading onto the teacup and saucer.

b Use a light to medium tone of pink and paint the rosebuds on the teacup and the small dots on the saucer. Add the leaves and stalks to the rosebuds with a pale tone of soft green; you may need to use the size 0 brush to paint the stalks.

c Add detail to the rosebuds with neat pink, and use neat dark green on the leaves to indicate shadows.

d Paint gold edges on the teacup and the saucer. ⟹

4 Method for painting the blue teacup and saucer

a Use a pale to medium tone of blue and the size 4 brush to paint shading onto the teacup and saucer.

b Use a medium tone of blue to paint the flowers on the teacup and saucer. Use this blue for the leaves and stalks too; switch to the size 0 brush if your stalks aren't fine enough.

c Paint a gold line around the centre ring of each saucer and on the handle and the bottom of the teacup. Paint gold dots on the lip of the teacup and the edge of the saucer.

5 Method for painting the yellow teacup and saucer

a Use a pale to medium tone of blue and with the size 4 brush paint shading onto the teacup and saucer.

b Paint yellow flowers on the teacup and saucer using a size 4 brush. Use a medium tone of pink for the smaller flowers, and paint the final few flowers using white. Give the white flowers a yellow centre. Paint the leaves using a medium tone of soft green.

c Add detail to the centre of the yellow petals using neat pink, and use this to add shading to the pink flowers. Add shading onto the leaves with dark green.

d Paint a gold line around the centre ring and edge of each saucer and on the teacup.

6 Leave all the elements to dry.

7 Turn the teacups over and lay a cocktail stick on the back of the shape (leave a small gap at the top, to make sure that the stick cannot be seen from the right side). Glue a ½ x ¾"/10 x 20 mm rectangle of modelling paste over the stick onto the back of the teacup. Leave it to dry.

8 Gently insert the cocktail stick of the teacup into the middle of the saucer; push down until the cup sits on the saucer. Place the cup and saucer on the cupcake.

9 If left at this stage, your cupcake will be perfectly charming. But if you want to add some extra interest to the cakes, then you can mirror the pattern that you have painted on the saucer around the edge of the cupcake, or even just add some gold dots.

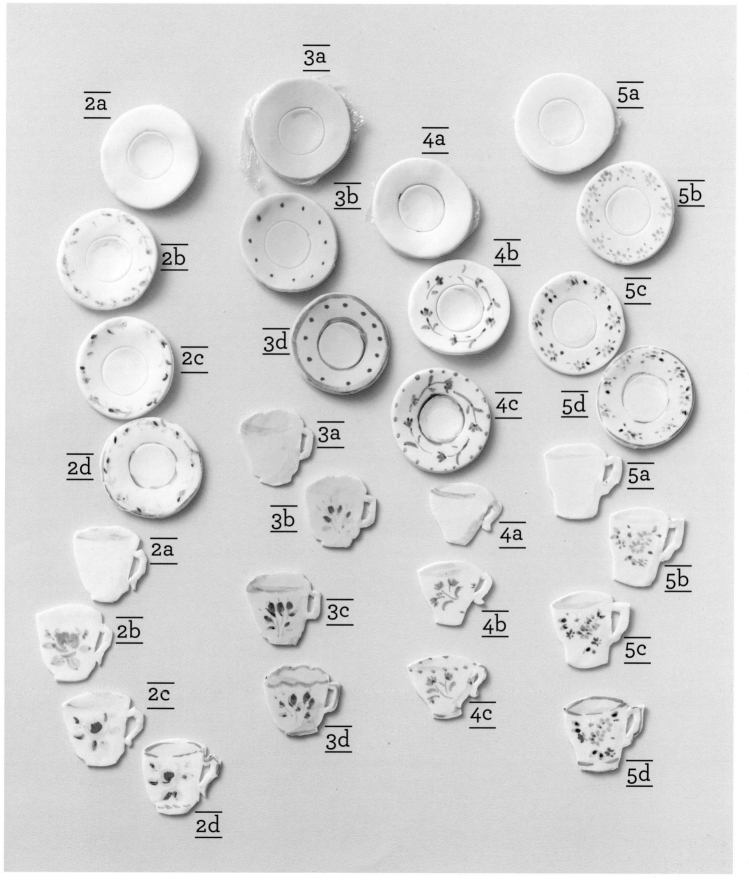

COOKIE PROJECTS

I love making cookies—maybe it's because of my childhood memories, maybe it's the joy of using my ever-increasing cookie cutter collection, or it could just be that I love eating them! (I really do *love* eating cookies.)

You will find cookie projects in this chapter to suit any skill level, so there's nothing to prevent you from baking up a storm and filling your kitchen with cookies. And because they have a long shelf life, you can make them well ahead of time.

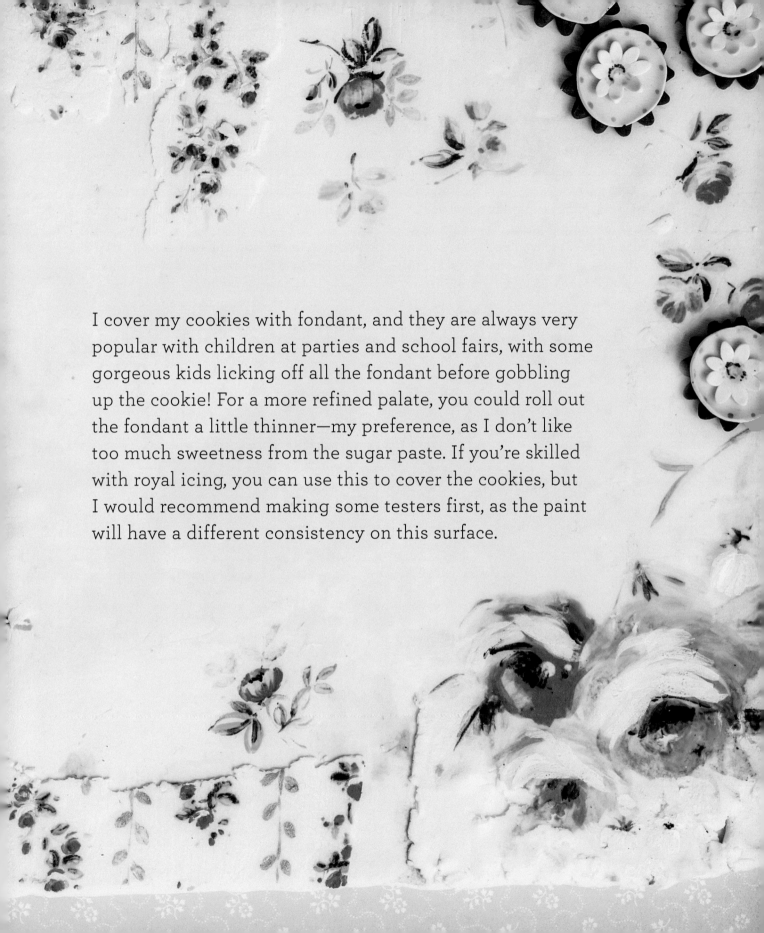

I cover my cookies with fondant, and they are always very popular with children at parties and school fairs, with some gorgeous kids licking off all the fondant before gobbling up the cookie! For a more refined palate, you could roll out the fondant a little thinner—my preference, as I don't like too much sweetness from the sugar paste. If you're skilled with royal icing, you can use this to cover the cookies, but I would recommend making some testers first, as the paint will have a different consistency on this surface.

MOUSTACHE COOKIES

I originally made these cookies for a friend's husband. He doesn't sport a moustache, nor, as far as I'm aware, does he aspire to. But for some reason my friend can't get enough handlebars, pencils, Dalis, or Fu Manchus to satisfy her moustache cravings. So she decided that he would have a full selection of moustaches for his birthday.

These cookies are really fun, and can double as party favours, but would also make great props for a photo booth, with the added bonus that you can eat them after the event!

EQUIPMENT

Paintbrush, size 0,
and a brush for gluing

1 lb 7 oz/650 g fondant

Confectioners' glue

Scalpel

¼"/5 mm spacers

30 cookie sticks

Colours

Brown, cream, orange

1 quantity of cookie dough

1 Roll out the dough using the spacers. Using the templates (*Templates 32-37, page 227*), cut out the dough to create the moustache shapes, making five of each design so you have 30 cookies. Gently insert a cookie stick into one side of each moustache, making sure that it does not come out the other side. Then turn the cookie over so that you can check the back; if you can see the stick coming through the surface, then take a small amount of dough and cover the exposed area. Turn them back the right way and place them on a tray lined with parchment paper, making sure that the sticks are lying flat, and chill them for at least 30 minutes. Bake in a preheated oven (190°C/375°F/Gas 5/170°C fan) for 8–10 minutes.

2 Divide the fondant into three and colour one-third light brown, one-third cream and the final third orange. Roll out the colours, one at a time, using the spacers, then turn the fondant over so you can stick the cookie on to the reverse side. Paint a cookie with the glue and stick it onto the fondant.

3 Using a scalpel, cut around the cookie.

4 Gently smooth the edges of the fondant with your fingers.

5 Leave the cookies overnight so that the fondant firms up.

6 Use the size 0 brush to paint in the details of the moustaches with brown paint.

7 Take pictures of yourself with the comedy moustaches and share on social media!

Cut out the cookies using the template

Paint glue onto the cookie

Press the cookie onto the fondant

Cut around the cookie

Smooth the edges

Paint the cookies

BUNNY COOKIES

These cookies would make a perfect Easter gift, or by adding name tags you can use them as place settings. But if you have bunny-obsessed children, then they are perfect all year round!

Don't worry if you can't find a cookie cutter that is exactly the same shape as the one that I have used. As long as it has a rabbit shape with large ears, it will be perfect.

EQUIPMENT

Paintbrush, sizes 8, 4, 0

Colours

Pink, white, blue, black

Bunny head-shaped cookies on lollipop sticks, covered in white fondant

1   Mix a small amount of white paint with baby blue and use the size 4 brush to paint two circles for the eyes. Leave the blue to dry completely before painting smaller black circles in the middle of the eyes. Paint a black triangle for the bunny's nose.

2   Mix together some white with a small amount of pink to create a pastel pink. With a very, very dry size 8 brush, paint the bunny's rosy cheeks, then with a slightly wetter size 0 brush and neat pink, add the mouth.

3   Add a few small dots of black at the sides of the mouth with the size 0 brush.

ROSE COOKIES

These are really simple cookies to paint, consisting of just one rose and a couple of leaves, but they are exceedingly pretty and will win you many, many compliments. Cover the cookies in a fondant that you have coloured a paler tone of the colour that you will be using for the rose. I am using purples here, but you could create a pink or a blue version, or even a rainbow of rose cookies!

EQUIPMENT

Paintbrush size 8

Tracing paper

Non-toxic pencil

Colours

Purple, soft green, dark green, white,

Round 3"/70 mm cookies covered in pale purple fondant

1. Enlarge the template for the Single Rose Cake (*Template 3, page 224*) by 110%, and transfer the design onto the prepared cookies using tracing paper. (Or if you prefer, this is a really easy design with which to practise your freehand painting technique.) You can add a few extra leaves, and don't be too concerned if some of the leaves don't fit onto the cookie (they will if your cookie has spread). But make sure the rose is in the centre of the design.

2. Use a pale purple tone and the size 8 brush to create the marks which form the rose petals. Paint in the leaves with a pale tone of the soft green.

3. Mix a medium purple tone and work some petals into the centre of the rose. Add some strokes of this colour on one side of the rose which will create the effect of shadow. Paint neat soft green onto the leaves, remembering to paint in the direction of the leaf veins.

4. On the light side of the rose, add a few strokes of white. You can also paint a few highlights of the white onto the leaves.

5. Add neat purple to the centre of the rose and paint a few strokes of this colour onto the main flower. Take care not to merge these marks, or you will pull the centre of the rose too far down. With the dark green, add lowlights to the leaves.

GOLD COOKIES

As discussed on page 153, there is no such thing as excessive use of gold in my work! So obviously I couldn't resist the urge to create a special gold cookie to add more than a little bling to any occasion.

The colour palette I've used for this project has a lovely vintage feel, but you could change it to create a different effect: soft pinks match especially well with gold, or you could even use a silver spray and paint with blue tones.

If the weather permits use the gold spray outside in the open. If not, use a homemade spray booth (see the instructions for the Gold Cake, page 153). You should always wear a protective mask whenever you use a spray can.

EQUIPMENT

Paintbrushes, sizes 8, 4

Tracing paper

Non-toxic pencil

1 x 3½ fl oz/100 ml can of edible gold spray

Colours

White, brown

Heart cookies (3¼"/80 mm wide) on a cookie stick, the cookies covered in light ochre-coloured fondant

1. This is a very simple design and is best painted freehand. But if you are not confident enough to do that, use the template (*Template 42, page 224*) to transfer the designs onto the prepared cookie with tracing paper.

2. Mix up a medium tone of brown and use to paint the flowers and the leaves with the size 8 brush—don't worry about being overly precise at this stage. Leave this layer of paint to dry.

3. Place the cookie in the spray booth (or on a large piece of scrap paper). Place a piece of paper over the cookie stick to keep it clean of any gold spray. Wearing a protective mask, apply a layer of gold spray. There should be a thick layer of gold, but you do need to be able to see a faint impression of the flowers and leaves underneath. If you feel that the layer of gold paint is not thick enough, add another layer once the first layer has dried.

4. Dip your size 8 brush into clean water and use it to remove any gold paint sitting on top of the flowers and leaves, but leave a small amount of gold in the centre of the two smaller flowers. Keep repeating the process until the area where the flowers and leaves are is clear (apart from the two centres). During this process, you will probably also remove most of the brown paint. Leave the cookie until the fondant has dried.

5. Use the white to paint in the flowers. Leave the centre of the largest one free from white, and leave the gold centres on the other two flowers.

6. Add a pale tone of brown into the centre of the large flower and, with the size 4 brush, paint the leaves using the same tone.

7. Use neat brown to darken the centre of the large flower and add some small dots around the centres of the other flowers. Finally, add detail to the leaves.

7

5,6

2

4

3

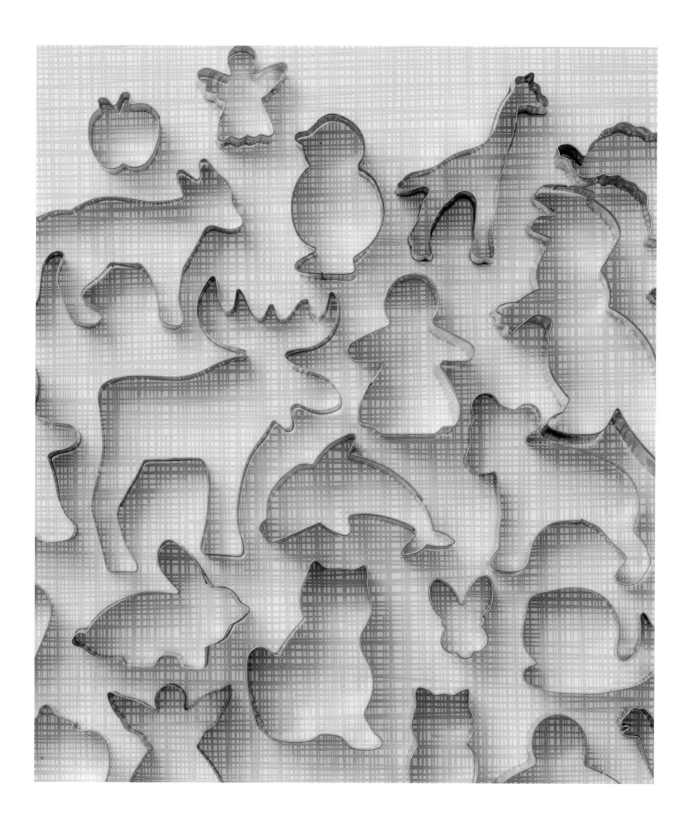

DAY OF THE DEAD COOKIES ● ● ●

I made these cookies for a friend's birthday. She has unusual tastes and I wanted to give her something beautiful. I love the contrast between the skull and the flowers. It speaks to me about the fragility of life . . . all painted on a tasty cookie!

Use the template provided to cut out your cookie, but you can reduce its size and create a whole family of different-sized skulls—mini ones would be great as party favours.

Take some time to experiment. You could use flowers from other projects to create different-looking designs. If you wanted a black skull, then paint the flowers onto white sugar paste, cut them out and stick them on the fondant-covered cookie.

You could also enlarge the template and create a head-turning skull cake. Just trim a cake into the shape of the skull using the template, cover with fondant and then paint the design in the manner described below. If you want to decorate the sides of the cake, then you could use some of the flowers from the main design.

EQUIPMENT

Paintbrushes, sizes 4, 0

Tracing paper

Non-toxic pencil

Colours

Pink, white, yellow, soft green, blue, brown

Cookies in the shape of the skull *(Template 38, page 228)* covered in white fondant (they will take around 20–25 minutes to bake as they are quite large)

1. Enlarge the template *(Template 38, page 228)* by 110%. Transfer the design onto the cookie using tracing paper, being careful not to lean on the fondant or press too hard with the pencil or you will create bumps and crevices in the surface.

2. Use a medium tone of pink and the size 4 brush and paint in the large pink flowers that are the skull's eyes. Remember to make each petal a slightly different shape, while being consistent with the size. Make sure to leave the centre of the flowers blank.

3. Use a medium tone of blue and paint the large blue flowers and the "nose." Again, leave the centres of the flowers blank and leave white spots on the blue nose. Don't worry if the spots aren't very round because you will be painting over them again with white paint.

4. Use a medium tone of brown to paint in the mouth and the eyebrows. Leave the teeth of the skull white and make sure that they are consistent in their size (you don't want a crooked smile).

5. With the size 0 brush and a medium tone of soft green, paint in the stalks. They should have lovely curvy lines, so take care not to be heavy-handed with these elements. It is fine to have a break in a line because it will just add to the natural effect (as natural as flowers on a skull can be!).

6. Switch back to the size 4 brush and paint in the small pink and yellow flowers in medium tones. Again, make sure that you leave unpainted ⟶

space in the centre of these flowers. Use these same tones to paint the centres of the large flowers, the flowers in the middle of the "nose," the outline of the mouth and the dots around the mouth.

7 Paint the leaves with a medium tone of soft green.

8 Add some detail onto the petals of the small yellow flowers using a medium tone of pink.

9 With neat pink, add some shading to the large and small pink flowers, again limiting this tone to just a few petals on each flower. Put a small dot of neat pink in the centre of each of the small yellow flowers.

10 Add shading to the blue flowers with neat blue. Add a dot of this colour to the centre of each of the small pink flowers and paint in a broken outline around the blue part of the "nose."

11 Use neat soft green to add shading to the leaves, and add a small amount to the centre of the large pink flowers. Don't paint this in a complete circle — leave a small amount of the white fondant peeking through.

12 With neat brown, add shading details to the leaves, the centres of the large flowers, the eyebrows and the teeth. Paint a broken outline around the green centres of the large pink flowers, then thin lines to represent the stamens with small dots of the brown at the end. You may need to change to the size 0 brush if the lines are too heavy—do not fill the centres with these lines.

13 Use white to paint in the teeth, and the dots on the "nose." You can also add some small dots around the centres of the large blue and pink flowers.

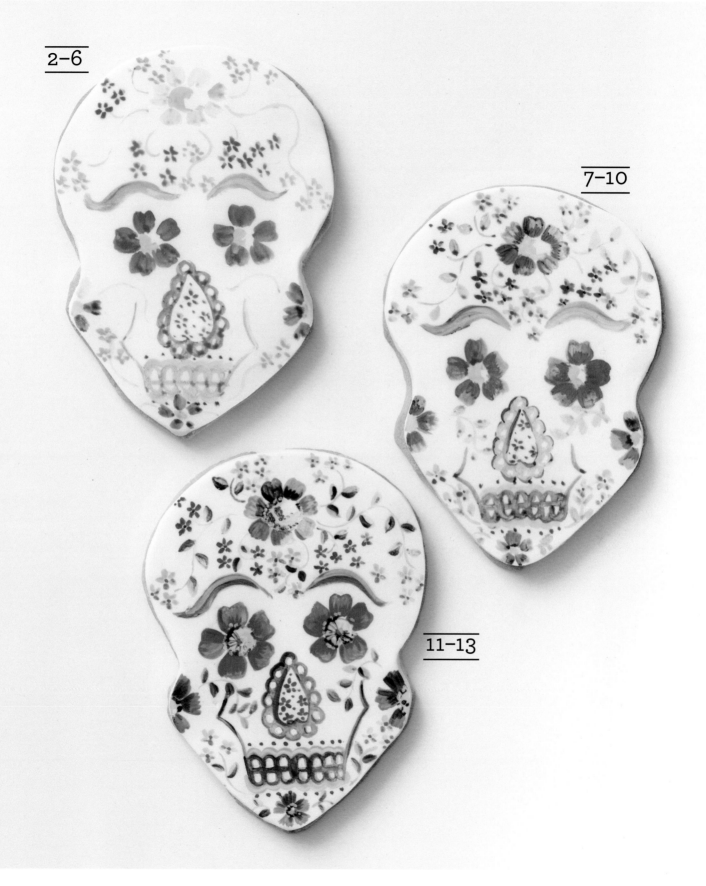

2-6

7-10

11-13

NAMED COOKIES ● ● ● ●

I often paint named cookies for wedding favours. They can be made with any shaped cookie cutter (for a bigger cookie, just enlarge the design to fit). I often use a rectangular cutter with a decorative edge—the shape mirrors a name-place card. But hearts or circles work well too—do a quick sketch of your composition first so you know how the elements will be placed on the shape.

Most of the designs are better painted freehand—when you trace small images onto fondant you lose the definition of the shape and the colours can become muddied. I make an exception for the bird design. Painting animals (or humans) freehand is difficult.

Before you start, spend time considering what typeface to use. No matter how careful you are, the names will always look hand-drawn, so don't choose a complicated typeface with lots of flourishes, or one that looks childish. I normally opt for a script style because it is easier to paint while keeping a nice flow (which makes it quicker to paint). If you're unsure, paint a few testers with different typefaces and then choose the one that looks the best.

I usually choose a typeface, then type out the alphabet in lower and upper cases. I refer to this while I paint the names freehand. But this takes some practice, so here are easier methods.

If you're confident in your handwriting skills, paint the name in your normal hand. I suggest that, first, you write the name on the cookie with a non-toxic pencil, then paint over it. This ensures the name fits neatly in the space, and is not squished at one end or runs into the flower.

Obviously there is a big difference in name lengths, ranging from the very short (Jon) to much longer (Geraldine). You can fit each name into the given space, so "Jon" is in larger letters than "Geraldine." Or you could fit the longest name into the space on the cookie to determine the type size, and print all the names out at the same size. It's a personal choice—I paint mine freehand, so normally fit the names to the space.

If you are too nervous to paint freehand, type the names in the correct sizes in a computer file and print out on printer-safe tracing paper. Reverse the tracing paper, gently trace over the letters, then turn the paper back over and trace the name onto a cookie.

EQUIPMENT

Paintbrushes, sizes 4, 0

Tracing paper

Non-toxic pencil

Colours

Purple, white, orange, yellow, soft green, dark green, brown

Cookies in your chosen shape, covered with ivory-coloured fondant

1 Method for painting the purple rose cookies

a Paint the rose head and buds with a size 4 brush and a medium tone of purple.

b Paint the stalk with the size 0 brush and a medium tone of soft green. Add the leaves in the same tone but switch back to the size 4 brush.

c Paint shadows in the centre of the rose and onto the buds with neat purple.

d Paint shading onto the leaves with dark green.

2 Method for painting the rosebud border cookies

a Paint the heads of the rosebuds a medium tone of orange with a size 4 brush.

b Paint the stalks with the size 0 brush and a medium tone of soft green. Add the leaves in the same tone, then switch back to the size 4 brush.

c Paint some shading onto the buds with neat orange.

d Paint shading onto the leaves with dark green. ⟹

3 Method for painting the forget-me-not cookies
a Paint the flowers using a light tone of purple with a size 4 brush.
b Paint the stalk with the size 0 brush and a medium tone of soft green. Add the leaves in the same tone but switch back to the size 4 brush.
c Paint some shading onto the petals with neat purple.
d Paint shading onto the leaves with dark green.
e Paint a dot in the centre of each flower with neat yellow.

4 Method for painting the blossom border cookies
a Paint the branches with a light tone of brown using the size 4 brush.
b Paint the blossoms with neat yellow and the leaves with light soft green.
c Use a medium tone of orange to add shading to some of the petals.
d Add a circle of neat orange in the centre of each flower.
e Add neat dark green shading to the leaves.
f With the size 0 brush and neat brown, paint detail onto the branches and in the centre of the blossoms.

5 Method for painting the bird cookies
a Trace the outline of the bird and branch onto the cookie using the template provided (*Template 39, page 226*) and tracing paper.
b Paint the branches with a light tone of brown using the size 4 brush.
c Paint the beak and belly of the bird with a medium tone of orange, and the back with yellow.
d Paint the blossoms with white, and add a few white strokes on the bird.
e Paint the centre of the blossoms with pink.
f Use neat brown and the size 0 brush to paint the outline of the bird. Add a few details for the wings and the eye. Add some detail to the branches and some in the centre of the blossoms.

6 Method for painting the pansy cookies
a With the size 4 brush, paint the bottom three petals of the pansy with yellow.
b Paint the top two petals with a light tone of purple, leaving a circle in the very middle of the flower that is not painted.
c Switch to the size 0 brush and paint the stalk with a medium tone of green. Use the size 4 brush to paint the leaves with the same tone.
d Paint details in the centre of the yellow petals with neat orange.
e With a medium tone of purple, add shading to the top two petals and paint a thin outline around the yellow petals (use the size 0 brush). Add some neat purple to the centre of the yellow petals.
f With dark green, paint the centre of the pansy and add shading to the leaves.

7 Paint the names on the cookies.

1a, b

1c, d

Jon

2a, b

2c, d

Sara

3a, b

3c-e

Brigitte

4a, b

4c-f

David

5a-e

5f

Amelie

6a-d

6e, f

Paul

CHEATS

The majority of my students are absolute beginners when it comes to painting on fondant, and they have not done any form of painting since their school days. They are often very anxious about trying a technique that takes them way outside their comfort zone. In a classroom environment, I can talk them through their worries and, at the end of the class, they emerge, blinking, carrying a painted cake that they are amazed they have produced by themselves.

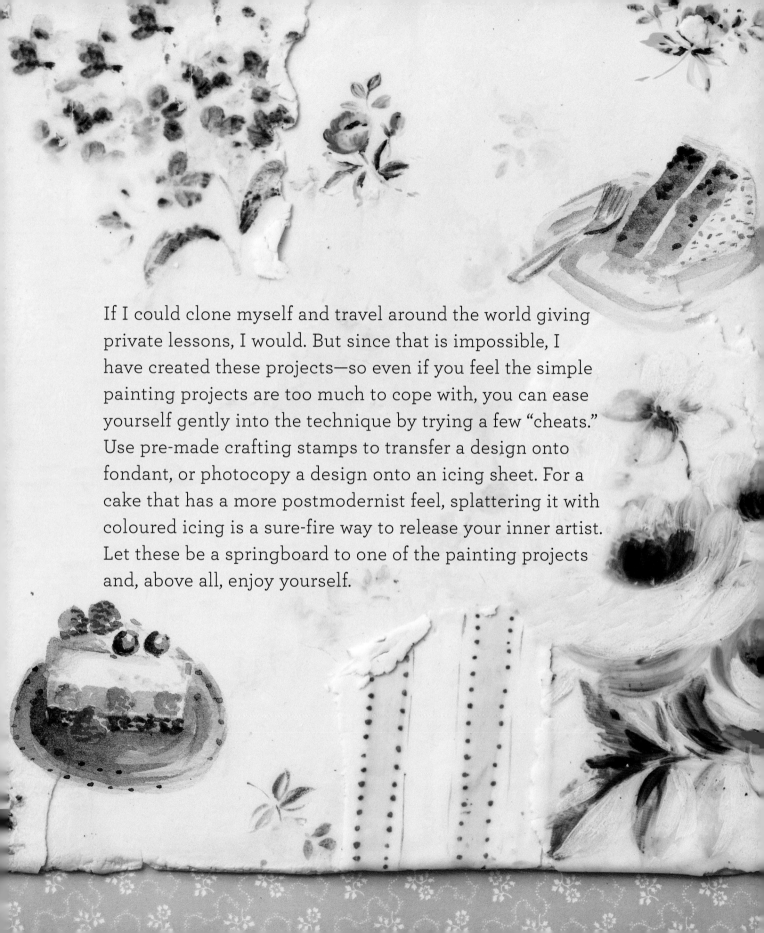

If I could clone myself and travel around the world giving private lessons, I would. But since that is impossible, I have created these projects—so even if you feel the simple painting projects are too much to cope with, you can ease yourself gently into the technique by trying a few "cheats." Use pre-made crafting stamps to transfer a design onto fondant, or photocopy a design onto an icing sheet. For a cake that has a more postmodernist feel, splattering it with coloured icing is a sure-fire way to release your inner artist. Let these be a springboard to one of the painting projects and, above all, enjoy yourself.

SPLATTER CAKE

For this project, you need to channel your inner Mark Rothko or Jackson Pollock by using abstract splatters of icing which create texture and interest (and a big helping of fun).

The splatters are really easy to create and you can use whatever implement you like to make them; I tried out a few ways and found a large ¾"/20 mm flat paintbrush was the best to use because it holds a decent amount of icing. I did try a spoon (not so good, more lumps than splatters) and a fork (acceptable). The trick is to really fling the paint and flick your wrist as you do it. This is a great cake to make if you're feeling angry, as it will release any pent-up tension you have!

This technique is incredibly messy, so cover the area you are working in with plastic sheets (although you will probably still find a blob of icing behind a radiator three months later). If you are too scared (or house-proud) to fling, you can always drizzle the colour over the cake.

I have created a colour palette for this project, but it would be incredibly easy to make your own that fits with the theme of the party. There are lots of websites that provide colour palettes and you can find unusual combinations—ones that also work beautifully together. Don't just stick to primary colours as the cake will look as if a pre-schooler has been at your icing; try using more sophisticated colours.

EQUIPMENT

A ¾"/20 mm flat brush (but any large paintbrush will be suitable)

A batch of royal icing

Colours
Soft green, pink, brown, blue, white

A three-tiered cake consisting of 10"/250 mm, 8"/200 mm, and 6"/150 mm cakes covered in white fondant

1 Mix up the royal icing, either using the recipe on page 67 or an instant packet mix. You may need to change the quantity of water slightly, as you require the icing to have the consistency of double cream. Divide the icing into five small bowls.

2 Mix up the pink colouring, which needs to be a medium to dark tone of pink. Take a teaspoon of this colour and add it to a bowl of the white icing and mix together to create the light pink. Make the aubergine colour by mixing pink and brown together—this should be your darkest tone. Make a medium tone of soft green icing. Colour the final batch of icing with a small amount of blue, then add some white powder to this to create a pastel colour.

3 Dip your paintbrush into one of the bowls and flick the colour onto the cake. The best way to do this is to bring your arm back with your elbow bent, then power your arm forward, bringing your elbow to the front and flicking your wrist. The more power you put into this move, the better your splatters. Try to change the angle of the splatters slightly, so that you don't end up with a series of vertical lines. (Or you can just drizzle the icing over the cake.)

4 Continue in the same manner until you have used every colour and the cake is finished to your satisfaction. If you find the colours are merging together on the cake and becoming muddy, then wait 5 or 10 minutes between applying each colour, to give the icing time to dry slightly.

PRINTED CAKE

I spend a fair amount of time dreaming about projects and most of the time I feel certain that they will be successful. However, with this project, I wasn't so sure. I wanted to create a beautiful design that you could print onto edible icing and use on a cake. But I was worried that it may look too twee (oh, the horror!), and it was only as the last piece was applied to the cake that I breathed a delighted sigh of relief. I still enjoy a buzz of pleasure when I see that a project is a winner.

You can easily change the feel of the cake by transferring a different print onto an icing sheet. Just make sure to use an image that has no copyright issues—certain vintage fabrics would be perfect, a photograph you have taken, or even a child's drawing.

Scan the template, enlarge it by 120% and then print it onto A4 edible icing sheets—you will need to print two sheets. If you don't have your own printer, I'm sure you can easily find somebody local with the facilities for edible printing. If not, there are many small businesses on the internet who offer this service.

The printed icing sheet should easily peel away from the backing sheet, but sometimes, if the sheet is too moist, you may find it harder to release. Here are a few helpful tips:

- Place the sheet in the freezer for 10–15 seconds, then peel off the backing.
- Put the sheet into a very low temperature oven for a few minutes, then peel off the backing.
- Blow a hairdryer on the back of the sheet for a minute, then peel off the backing.

If you find that the icing sheet is crumbling and cracking as you release it from its backing, then it has dried out too much and you will need to reprint it.

EQUIPMENT

Large flat brush to moisten the fondant

Two printed icing sheets of the floral design template (*Template 40, page 231*)

6"/150 mm square cake covered in white fondant

1   Make a paper template for the top of the cake, and one for the sides. I have not given you measurements for this, as each cake will differ slightly depending on the thickness of your buttercream and fondant. So, by making your own template, you will create a better fitting covering.

2   One printed sheet will be big enough to cut out three sides, separately rather than in one long strip. The other sheet will give you the final side and the top of the cake. Don't peel the backing off the printed sheets until you are about to put them on the cake, or the icing could dry out and crack.

3   Lightly moisten one side of the cake at a time (don't wet the cake, or the sheet can become too soggy and tear when you stick it to the cake). Peel off the backing and stick the icing sheet to the side. Smooth down all the edges with paper towels. Repeat for all the sides.

4   Moisten the top of the cake, peel off the backing for the top piece and stick it down on the cake. Smooth down all the edges.

PAINT-BY-NUMBERS

If you want to paint on fondant but are too nervous to start, this project is a great way of easing yourself in gently. Paint-by-numbers is something I'm sure you played with as a child, you might have been given a kit by your grandma or aunt, and, if your mum is anything like mine, the result still hangs proudly on a wall somewhere!

I have created a design for you in the traditional paint-by-numbers manner, and what could be more traditional than a winter scene with deer?

If you enjoy this way of painting, you could always create your own paint-by-numbers design. Draw out your design onto paper, trace over the lines with a thicker black pen, and then rub out the pencil. Scan your design and print it onto edible icing sheets. You could even make paint-by-numbers cupcake toppers for a DIY party favour.

EQUIPMENT

Paintbrush, size 4, plus size 4 brush for gluing

Large flat brush to moisten the fondant

1¾ oz/50 g brown fondant

Confectioner's glue

Scalpel

Extruder (optional)

Colours

Orange, white, dark green, blue, brown

Printed icing sheet of the paint-by-numbers template (*Template 41, page 229*), template enlarged by 115%

An 8"/200 mm cake with 1"/25 mm cut off one of the sides to create an 8 x 7"/200 x 180 mm cake, covered in white fondant

1. Trim the printed icing sheet to the size of the cake (8 x 7"/200 x 180 mm).

2. Brush a small amount of boiled water on top of the cake—it should be slightly moistened rather than wet.

3. Peel the icing sheet from its backing and place it on top of the cake (see the Printed Cake project, pages 210–11).

4. Mix up the colours according to the chart on page 214. It is best to mix all the colour you need at the start, to prevent the tones changing as you paint. Adding white to the colours gives them a more opaque quality, which looks more like the oil paints or gouache traditionally used for paint-by-numbers.

   Blue—add a small amount of white to the blue.
   Pale blue—add a small amount of blue to the white.
   Orange—mix together orange and a small amount of white.
   Dark brown—mix together brown with a small amount of white.
   Light brown—mix together white with brown and orange.
   Green—mix together dark green with a small amount of white.

5. Paint the picture with the size 4 brush, matching your colours to the colour spots on the design.

6. Roll out the brown fondant into a long thin sausage (or use an extruder) and glue it around the edge of the icing sheet. Trim the joins with a scalpel.

7. You can leave the cake as it is, or tie a ribbon around the sides, or—if you are feeling very daring—paint your own design!

Colours to use

Paint glue on the edge of the cake

Extrude a ribbon of fondant

Overlap the fondant at the corners

Continue the fondant around all sides

Trim the joins

LOVE HEARTS

While it is a given that these cookies would make a fabulous Valentine's Day present, they are perfect for any occasion when you want to express your love and devotion to someone special. Or you could create a thank-you cookie to give to someone who has gone that extra mile.

Make sure that the stamps you use for this project are new. Clean them in soapy water before you use them (make sure they are completely dry before stamping), and keep them solely for cake-decorating projects.

EQUIPMENT

Paintbrush, size 4, and a brush for gluing

1 lb 10 oz/750 g fondant

Confectioners' glue

Circle cutter about 2¾-3¼"/70-80 mm (same one used for cookies)

A heart cutter small enough to fit inside the fondant circle but still large enough to allow enough room for the lettering

An alphabet stamp set

Colours

Soft green, pink, orange, yellow

20 cookies, cut into circles about 2¾-3¼"/70-80 mm

1. Colour 5½ oz/150 g of the fondant pale pink, 5½ oz/150 g pale green, 5½ oz/150 g pale yellow and 5½ oz/150 g pale orange; leave the remaining fondant white. Use a cocktail stick to introduce the colour gradually to the fondant, so that you don't overcolour it and make it too dark—you want to achieve beautiful pastel tones.

2. Roll out the fondant to an even thickness of ⅛-¼"/3-4 mm (or use the spacers). Cut out circles and glue the fondant circles to the cookies. You do not need to leave the fondant to dry out for this project—you can print onto it immediately.

3. Paint neat pink onto the edge of the heart cutter—I use the wrong side (not the side you would use to cut out) as it has a thicker edge.

4. Gently press the painted edge onto the fondant-covered cookie.

5. Decide on the motto you want to press into the cookie. Using the alphabet stamps, start by printing the middle letter of the word (for the first word, if you have more than one). So, if you want to print "tweet me," with "tweet" on the first line, choose the letter "e," print this in line with the middle of the heart, and then add the letters "tw" and "et" on either side: working outwards, print "w" first and then "t," then, on the other side, "e" first and then "t." This makes sure that you don't have a lopsided message. If you have an even-lettered word such as "gorgeous," obviously there is no middle letter—the centre of the word is the space between the "g" and the "e." So choose the letter nearest the space, in this case the "g," and place it slightly to the left of the centre of the heart, then proceed with the method described above.

6. Leave the cookies to dry before you give them to your loved one(s)—and then bask in their happiness!

Paint pink onto the heart cutter

Gently press it into the cookie

Don't worry if the lines are broken

Paint the alphabet stamps

Press them gently onto the cookie

STAMPED COOKIES

This is a similar technique to the Love Hearts (page 217), but instead of alphabet stamps, you use picture stamps. You can easily pick these up from an art or craft shop or from an online specialist. There are a myriad of stamps available in every conceivable shape and theme, however you do need to use a fairly simple image. A stamp with excessive shading or detailing will make it hard to print out a nice clean image (this is because the edible paints we are using are a different consistency from printing inks).

When choosing a cookie shape to match your stamp, think about the final product. After the stamp has been applied to the fondant, there should be a suitable gap between the image and the edge of the cookie (although it can be nice to offset the stamp on the cookie too). However, you don't want the image to be lost in the centre of the cookie. I normally take my cookie cutters and hold them in front of the stamp before I commit to a shape, so that I can get a rough idea of how the two will work together.

Here is a sentence that I rarely say, but in this case, ignore my previous advice (about leaving the cookie to dry). The stamp will work best if there is still some give to the fondant—in fact, it is preferable to stamp cookies as soon as you've covered them. You must make sure that the fondant is perfectly flat, so that the impression of the whole stamp is printed. If you have any bumps or dents, you will miss areas of the image. Using the spacers will help to keep the fondant quite thick, or roll it out to an even ¼"/5 mm thickness.

If your cookies are quite bumpy, then turn them over and cover the back with the fondant (this side should be quite flat because it was against the surface of the baking tray). Then, once the fondant has been applied to the cookie, smooth over the top with the smoothers to ensure a perfectly flat finish.

EQUIPMENT

Paintbrush, size 8

Craft stamps

Colours

Blue, white

Cookies in your chosen shapes, covered in ivory-coloured fondant

1. Mix a small amount of blue and white together (the white dries the colour out a little, which stops it spreading when printed).

2. Paint the colour onto the stamp, making sure that there isn't any excess colour on the flat part of the stamp, as this can transfer onto the cookie.

3. Turn the stamp over and hold it above the cookie while you check the positioning.

4. Carefully press the stamp into the fondant.

5. Gently lift the stamp off the cookie, and voila! A perfectly printed image.

Mix the white and blue paints together

Paint the colour onto the stamp

The painted stamp

Position the stamp on the cookie

Press down gently

TEMPLATES

template 42

template 25

template 1

template 2

template 3

template 26

template 27

template 4

template 6

template 5

template 7

template 39

template 24

template 28

template 29

template 30

template 31

template 32

template 33

template 34

template 35

template 36

template 37

templates 14 & 15

template 13

template 38

templates 8–12

template 16

template 17

template 18

template 19

template 21

template 20

template 22

template 23

INDEX

Acknowledgments

There are so many people without whom this book would still be a pipe dream, and I cannot let this opportunity go by without acknowledging them.

Thank you to my agent Claire Hulton, who believed in *The Painted Cake* from the beginning. I certainly could not have done this without her; she is a real gem and I am truly grateful to her.

There are many people at Murdoch Books who have had a hand in this book. I have to especially thank Diana Hill, my fabulous publisher, who has held my hand and graciously led me through my first foray into publishing. Thanks to Miriam Steenhauer and Claire Grady who patiently put up with all my questions and queries, and Virginia Birch who picked up the baton and ran with it. Thanks to Holly O'Neill for editing the manuscript and wading through my grammar and spelling mistakes, and a special thanks must go to Emilia Toia, who has designed a really beautiful book that complements the projects to perfection.

It was an absolute pleasure to work with such an amazing photographer as Nathan Pask. He made what could have been a very stressful time massively fun, and I am ecstatic with the images he created — I feel lucky to have had him as part of "Team Cake." I also must thank the team at Snap Studios, especially Steph King, who looked after us so well while we were shooting. And a big thank you to Sharon Herholdt, for making my baker's nails look beautiful!

I have to thank some wonderful suppliers for helping me source lovely props for the photoshoot: Marie Kitchen from Heartfelt Handmade; Vicky Trainer from The Linen Garden (for some gorgeous cloths and lacey bits); Reilly and Moss (for some stunning cake stands) and Baker and Maker for many fabulous props. There are also some local suppliers from my hometown, Berkhamsted, to thank: Custom Kitchens for loaning me a gorgeous worktop, Petals Flower Shop for some beautiful flowers and Peter John Interiors for all the lovely wallpaper. And thank you to Kate from Cakeadoodledo for my spotty apron.

There are also many, many friends who deserve a special thank you for helping me out while I was writing the book, especially for looking after my kidlets and for acting as chauffeurs while I was up to my eyes in buttercream. I must also mention Emma Thomas: thank you for all the cakey fun we've had in the last few years, it's been a blast.

It may seem strange (considering that I have just written this book!) but I am not great with words— I'm much more of a visual person. So it is very difficult to verbalise the thanks I have saved for the most important people in my life. Hopefully the rest of the book will speak for that, but I will try my best to thank them here.

Without my parents' encouragement and love I would never have been able to pursue a career as an artist. They have always been gracious and selfless in caring for me—and now, their grandchildren—and they have backed me all the way. Thank you both. x

I now have two mini-artists of my own, and I want to thank my lovely girls for their patience and encouragement. Without you, I would never have started down this particular path—you are both my inspiration and joy.

Finally, a huge thank you to Paul, my fabulous husband. You have helped make this all possible. From the very start, you were there, helping me out with your amazing ninja grammar and vocabulary skills. You have patiently dealt with a house full of cake and icing. You have endured many, many conversations about cake with good humour, and you always make me laugh.

Thank you, Mr. Lemon Drizzle! xx

Skyhorse Publishing books may be purchased in bulk at special discounts for sales promotion, corporate gifts, fund-raising, or educational purposes. Special editions can also be created to specifications. For details, contact the Special Sales Department, Skyhorse Publishing, 307 West 36th Street, 11th Floor, New York, NY 10018 or info@skyhorsepublishing.com.

Skyhorse® and Skyhorse Publishing® are registered trademarks of Skyhorse Publishing, Inc.®, a Delaware corporation.

Visit our website at www.skyhorsepublishing.com.

10 9 8 7 6 5 4 3 2

Library of Congress Cataloging-in-Publication Data is available on file.

IMPORTANT: Those who might be at risk from the effects of salmonella poisoning (the elderly, pregnant women, young children, and those suffering from immune deficiency diseases) should consult their doctor before eating raw eggs.

OVEN GUIDE: You may find cooking times vary depending on the oven you are using. For fan-forced ovens, as a general rule, set the oven temperature to 20°C (35°F) lower than indicated in the recipe.

MEASUREMENTS GUIDE: We have used 20 ml (4 teaspoon) tablespoon measures. If you are using a 15 ml (3 teaspoon) tablespoon (standard US tablespoon), add an extra teaspoon of the ingredient for each tablespoon specified.

Print ISBN: 978-1-5107-0488-6
Ebook ISBN: 978-1-5107-0491-6

Printed in China